ADR DESKBOOK for the BUSINESS LAWYER

A Cross-Disciplinary Workbook

F. PETER PHILLIPS, EDITOR

AMERICAN BAR ASSOCIATION
Business Law Section

Cover design by Jill Tedhams/ABA Design

Page layout by Quadrum Solutions.

Printed in the United States of America.

20 19 18 17 16   5 4 3 2 1

Library of Congress Cataloging-in-Publication Data

Names: Phillips, F. Peter, editor.
Title: ADR deskbook for business lawyers / F. Peter Phillips, editor.
Description: Chicago, Illinois : American Bar Association, 2016. | Includes index.
Identifiers: LCCN 2016001354 (print) | LCCN 2016001480 (ebook) | ISBN 9781634254755 (pbk. : alk. paper) | ISBN 9781634254762 ()
Subjects: LCSH: Dispute resolution (Law)—United States.
Classification: LCC KF9084 .A93 2016 (print) | LCC KF9084 (ebook) | DDC 347.73/9—dc23
LC record available at http://lccn.loc.gov/2016001354

Discounts are available for books ordered in bulk. Special consideration is given to state bars, CLE programs, and other bar-related organizations. Inquire at Book Publishing, ABA Publishing, American Bar Association, 321 N. Clark Street, Chicago, Illinois 60654-7598.

www.shopABA.org

With thanks for their perseverance, to:

E.B.

P.B.P.

J.K.B.P.

Contents

Acknowledgments

The ABA Business Law Section and the Editor of this book wish to acknowledge and thank Barb Kallusky, Assistant Director, Public Services of the Warren E. Burger Library at Mitchell Hamline School of Law for her work cite checking this book.

The Editor also wishes to acknowledge the participation of the contributing authors; the support of the members of the ABA Business Law Section Committee on Dispute Resolution; and the expertise and patience of Prof. Sharon Sandeen of Mitchell Hamline School of Law, whose service on the Business Law Section Publications Board is deeply valued.

Foreword

Paulette Brown

The practice of law is rapidly changing in many ways. Along with the innovations in technology, regulation, marketing, billing, ethics, and client expectations, lawyers have recently confronted another tectonic shift: What Marc Galanter calls the "Vanishing Trial."[1]

The world we lived in as children treated trials as the pinnacle of legal practice: Atticus Finch in *To Kill a Mockingbird*, spontaneous confessions of guilt in *Perry Mason*, searing cross-examinations in *Law & Order*. Yet, in my own state of New Jersey, fully 99% of civil cases filed are disposed of by means other than verdict at trial.[2] Some are withdrawn; some are dismissed through dispositive motion; many are settled. But, few are tried.

This trend is only the tip of the iceberg, when one considers all of the civil disputes that were not filed in the first instance. Consider all of the commercial disagreements, the neighbor-to-neighbor conflicts, the insurance claims, the online consumer orders, the employment conflicts, that were adjusted or negotiated or resolved before any court was called in to adjudicate. And there are, in addition, all the securities disputes, the reinsurance battles, the labor disputes, and others that were sent to arbitration rather than to court.

If yesterday's lawyer gave impassioned closing arguments to a rapt jury, today's lawyer better assists her client by intentionally avoiding lengthy, costly, and uncertain processes like trial, and spends time fixing the problem. The old model was lawyer as vindicator. The new model is the lawyer as problem-solver.

It is all the more appropriate, therefore, that the American Bar Association Business Law Section offer this volume. Covering several

---

1. Marc Galanter, *The Vanishing Trial: An Examination of Trials and Related Matters in Federal and State Courts*, 1 J. Empirical Legal Stud., 459 (2004).

2. *See* New Jersey Judiciary Civil Statistics June 2015 (http://www.judiciary.state.nj.us/quant/gray1506.pdf), at 89.

fields of business law, the essays in this book guide practitioners in how Alternative Dispute Resolution (ADR) is currently used to realign parties' commercial interests and manage disputes in a way that is commercially rational, and of benefit to the clients we serve. I particularly encourage readers to take seriously the guides for transactional drafting, for embedding dispute systems into the commercial enterprise, and for looking ahead to forms of mediation and arbitration that return us to the essential, direct, and straightforward way of helping clients do business efficiently. The glossary offered in Chapter 4 is a particularly useful tool for all practitioners, ensuring that we converse with each other accurately and with a minimum of misunderstanding.

As lawyers, whether as transactional or litigating counsel, we negotiate and cut deals on behalf of our clients. In light of the Vanishing Trial, perhaps it is time to take the word "Alternative" out of ADR. This is now a mainstream practice area, and competence in these skills will soon be a core client expectation. I welcome the publication of this volume and look forward to its future enhancement and enlargement to even more fields of practice.

PART 1

Theory

An Introduction to Principled Negotiation, Client Representation in Mediation, and the Arbitration Process

F. Peter Phillips

EDITOR'S NOTE: The first four chapters of this Workbook provide an introduction to the topic of business dispute anticipation and resolution that does not involve resort to the public courts. In this chapter, the three main categories of ADR—negotiation, mediation, and arbitration—are defined and explained in general terms, and the stage is set for more specific application of the principles of nonjudicial dispute resolution.

There are no perfect contracts. Therefore, it is to be expected that, at some point during the life of a project, parties to business agreements will need to reformulate the terms of their deals. Usually, this takes place by assent, to the benefit of the deal and the mutual advantage of the parties. Sometimes it doesn't.

An aggrieved party to a business deal ordinarily makes every effort to rectify the situation prior to asserting a legal claim for damages. It's perfectly understandable why that should be. Legal proceedings distract businesspeople from their jobs. They cost money. They take time. Their outcome is uncertain and legally (rather than commercially) structured. Legal proceedings often lack finality as the losing party seeks appellate review. Relationships go very sour very fast. In short, very few businesspeople make money suing their business partners.

Alternative Dispute Resolution, or ADR, was initially an effort to devise ways to resolve business conflicts that minimized or eliminated the need to go to court. The practice has become so mainstreamed, however, that it's hardly an alternative any more—it's the way most people do business. When you consider how many disputes are resolved through discussion or negotiation and never ripen into legal claims, you realize that fixing problems is usually more profitable than vindicating contractual rights. Then consider that of the 273,312 civil cases filed in U.S. District Courts in the 12 months ended June 15, 2015, only 2,935 of them—1.1%—were disposed by trial, and you appreciate that business disputes simply don't get resolved in court. They get resolved by what we used to call "alternative" dispute resolution.

Business lawyers are, nevertheless, essential players in business conflict management and resolution. But to best serve their clients, business lawyers might need a slight shift in focus. A transactional counselor may stuff a contract full of warranties, reps, and assurances—but the contract still has no value unless those promises can be effectively enforced by means of a dispute resolution clause. A dispute resolution expert who (as I was trained to do) examines a client's contract for rights, defenses, statutes of limitations, fraud, and other causes of action might also spend time understanding what the client initially wanted out of the joint venture and how best to negotiate a resolution that achieves it.

Classically, ADR is divided into three "baskets": Negotiation, Mediation and Arbitration. The first two result in consensual outcomes whose terms are determined by the parties themselves. The third is an adjudicative process, the outcome of which is determined by a third-party and is final and binding upon the disputants. Here are some rudimentary features of each ADR process.

Negotiation

Considering the fundamental role that legal negotiation plays in rendering legal services, it is surprising that until very recently, few law schools offered training in the skill. Even today, not a single law school includes a stand-alone course in negotiation skills in its list of courses required for graduation. This despite negotiation's being at the core of real estate, bankruptcy, deal making, securities, sales, tax disputes, legislation, administrative regulation, alternate corporate vehicle formation, and—as noted above—dispute resolution.

Negotiation styles and strategies can be understood in at least three polarities. "Adversarial vs. Collaborative" bargaining compares negotiators who trade proposals like tennis players volley with negotiators who invite joint problem solving like a group working on a jigsaw puzzle at a beach house. "Distributive vs. Integrative" bargaining refers to processes designed to allocate (and therefore compete for) a fixed value, like pennies on a table, as opposed to bargaining strategies that are susceptible to value-adding components, as when in raise negotiation, sources of value include not only dollars but also flex time, vacation time, retirement benefits, or healthcare. "Interest-based vs. Positional" bargaining compares negotiators who assess various offers and demands in an effort to obtain the underlying objective of the principal to negotiators who exchange bid-ask-bid-ask and end up somewhere between their initial positions.

No one approach is suitable for every negotiation. And in any event, there is no right and wrong in negotiation. Nevertheless, both scholars and experienced practitioners tend to agree that interest-based bargaining tends to yield more nuanced and commercially robust outcomes; that integrative bargaining tends to yield outcomes that benefit both parties; and that collaborative bargaining tends to repair and even improve business and professional relationships, both between the principals and their lawyer agents.

Many untrained negotiators approach the deal table prepared with a list of demands and justifications, including alternative proposals and reservation points, eager to take control. Perhaps ironically, the most experienced negotiators listen far more than they speak. Preparing for a negotiation involves determining what your client wants, what he or she is willing to do to get it, and what the alternative is in the event that the negotiation fails. But learning what the counterparty wants and thinking up ways that your client's objectives can be attained on terms that the other party consents to—that is much of the art of successful negotiation.

In this "dance," the skilled negotiator knows when to reveal and when to withhold, when to concede and when to seek reciprocation, when to assert what's important to a client and when to misdirect an adversary with respect to priorities, and when to agree to a component of a multifaceted deal and when to hold it in abeyance pending the resolution (often through trade-offs and exchanges) of the entire deal. And the negotiator knows how to do all of this in an ethical manner.

Negotiation literature is very, very robust, and the challenge of finding a negotiating style that works is every lawyer's White Whale. But the fundamental enticement is the lure of Sherlock Holmes's "dog that didn't bark." Negotiators seek the lawsuit that wasn't filed, the business divorce without recriminations, the problem that never ripened into a conflict, the conflict that never ripened into a dispute.

Mediation

Mediation is negotiation with adult supervision. Negotiators who reach an impasse in resolving the problem to their clients' mutual satisfaction are often well advised to bring in a mediator to test whether what looks like an impasse is, at heart, the product of mistrust, miscommunication, an inability to recognize mutually beneficial prospects, or an understandable lack of candor.

Mediators are injected into a negotiation on certain terms. First, they are equally trusted by both parties to the negotiation. Second, they promise that they will not reveal information learned from one party without that party's permission. Third, they extract from the participants an undertaking that nothing communicated during the process can be used in subsequent litigation—information and statements in mediation are not only confidential, but privileged. And fourth, they are skilled at listening, probing, reality testing, detecting interests that lie beneath positions, and steering the parties towards "yes."

Some mediators see themselves as the person who enters a dispute over a group of oranges, and who comes to learn that one party wants the peel and the other the pulp and therefore both sides' interests can be met. Some see themselves as moderators of emotional behavior, allowing venting and suggesting a cooler analysis, sometimes at the behest of a client's own attorney. The most appealing and simplest image of a mediator may be of the wise old woman who privately visits two estranged young lovers, one at a time. Each of the angry, hurt people confides in her the reasons for their estrangement, and it takes very little time before the old woman has more information, insight, and understanding than either of the two young people. She is in a position to help because she knows things about them both that neither one knows about the other—including ways they can make each other happier than they would be alone.

This role of the "trusted mandarin" is one of the essential attributes of mediation, and the reason so many commercial mediations result in agreement where direct negotiation failed. The mediator soon knows the deal better than each party and is possessed of information and analysis that each party cannot possibly possess because—through caution, distrust, or negotiation strategy—they were not privy to it to the degree the mediator is. The mediator can develop an understanding of critical negotiation components—underlying business objectives, possibilities for mutual gain, the necessity of modification of terms—that can serve to lead the parties to robust commercial outcomes. And suggestions or queries (or even challenges) that come from the mediator are usually more attentively received than the same words coming from a counterparty.

One of the most frustrating things an ADR practitioner can hear is that counsel does not want to engage in mediation "because the mediator always splits the baby." As we will see below, it is arbitrators who possess the authority to adjudicate a dispute, rendering a final and binding award that is not susceptible to review on the merits and that is enforceable in courts in the United States and abroad. A mediator, by contrast, is a weird combination of a counselor and a midwife. In mediation, it is the parties, not the neutral, who devise and agree upon a commercially rational outcome. To paraphrase James Joyce, upon the successful conclusion of a mediation, the mediator refines herself out of existence.

Arbitration

Arbitration is an adjudicative process resulting from the parties' contractual agreement to waive any right to assert claims in a judicial forum and instead to engage a mutually selected private party to hear evidence and issue a final, binding and non-appealable decision on the merits of the dispute.

Arbitration is of centuries' lineage. No doubt a Phoenician merchant, dissatisfied with the quality of cotton he was being offered by an Egyptian seller, agreed to abide by the decision of an old wizened cotton merchant there on the wharf. Arbitration in such an instance illustrates the fundamental features of the process—it is mercantile; it is fast; it is reliable; it involves a private adjudicator selected by the parties for his knowledge of the business rather than the law; and it allows busy merchants to go on their way without being diverted by lengthy, costly, and uncertain judicial proceedings.

You wouldn't know it to read the newspapers, but modern commercial arbitrations continue this tradition without serious disruption or challenge. Every month hundreds, even thousands of business disputes are resolved by final and binding arbitration under the rules of the American Arbitration Association, the Singapore International Arbitration Centre, JAMS, the Hong Kong International Arbitration Centre, the London Centre for International Arbitration, the International Chamber of Commerce, CPR Institute, and many other reputable providers of arbitration services. Agreements to arbitrate rather than litigate are negotiated; demands for arbitration are served and answered; arbitral awards are issued and complied with, all in service of the commercial objectives of the parties. In the United States, entire industries use arbitration as the exclusive means of resolving disputes—including securities and major league athletics.

The practice is not abstruse. The Commercial Rules of the American Arbitration Association are readily available and describe a straightforward method of conducting an arbitration; the process averages well under a year from assertion of a claim to issuance of an award. By their agreements, parties can customize the process as they see fit—setting forth qualifications for arbitrators, determining what law or rules shall govern the contract and the arbitration, limiting or expanding prehearing exchange of information, providing for efficient exchange or joint testimony of experts, and so on. Arbitration is a creature of contract, and an agreement to arbitrate will be enforced by American courts unless attacked on grounds applicable to the enforceability of any contract.

American arbitration law is currently wrestling with important questions of policy. Are agreements to arbitrate enforceable against consumers who are unaware of the existence or import of the agreements? Are provisions of arbitration agreements purporting to prohibit collective redress enforceable? What is the relationship between state consumer protection laws and federal judicial policies favoring arbitration? Who decides these questions, the arbitrator selected by the parties or a court seized of a motion to compel arbitration or to vacate or enforce an arbitrator's award? Has the litigation that sometimes surrounds arbitration procedures rendered the process as costly and time-consuming as litigation would have been in the first place?

These challenges are, for the most part, around the edges of the envelope of private dispute resolution. For the purposes of this introductory essay, practitioners should approach arbitration with a degree of confidence borne of centuries of commercial usage. Though arbitral awards may not be appealed, the finality they promise often has commercial value. Though court judgments may not be recognized outside the jurisdictions that issued them, arbitral awards are enforceable in almost 200 countries by operation of the New York Convention. Though courts are public forums, arbitration hearings (and, usually, arbitration awards) are confidential. And while courts randomly assign the judge who will preside over the dispute, parties to arbitration select the adjudicator based on predetermined criteria and can demand an award that reflects not only the law, but also standard practices in the industry and other relief that a court may not be empowered to render.

Of course, methods of dispute resolution are as many and varied as the human mind can conjure. Counsel might consider variants of consensual non-binding processes, such as conducting a mini-trial before senior executives of the disputing companies, seeking a non-binding evaluation of the claims and defenses from a retired and trusted jurist, or asking a mediator to propose an outcome in the event that parties cannot reach agreement during mediation. They can come to a side agreement that will conform an arbitrator's award to a number within pre-agreed boundaries. Indeed, in the chapters that follow, several examples of ingenious methods of commercial dispute resolution processes are described, the product in each case of the particular needs of a particular industry or commercial application.

One hopes that with this general introduction, the reader can intelligently discuss pre-dispute contractual provisions in deals that are designed to preserve the value of the transaction and also discuss with a client or a counterparty the fastest, cheapest and most appropriate way to resolve a commercial dispute once it has presented itself.

CHAPTER 2

Tips on Preparing for Mediation

Sylvia Mayer

EDITOR'S NOTE: Mediation is uniquely client-directed. Yet without professional guidance few business clients are in a position to comprehend the benefits and risks of entering into mediation, the success of which depends on informed client engagement. In this chapter, Sylvia Mayer offers some practical pointers for getting a client ready for mediation.

In many jurisdictions, mediation of civil lawsuits falls into the same category as death and taxes—it is a certainty. Mediation can also be used to resolve prelitigation disputes and to bridge past an impasse in business dealings.

While few attorneys would go to trial unprepared, many attorneys do not realize that it is equally important to prepare for mediation. As discussed in greater detail below, preparation includes analysis of the strengths and weaknesses of your case, preparation of your client, and determination of your best alternative to a negotiated agreement ("BATNA") and worst alternative to a negotiated agreement ("WATNA").

Ben Franklin had it right when he said, "By failing to prepare, you are preparing to fail."[1] With this in mind, here are five practical tips to help you prepare to succeed at mediation.

---

1. *See* http://www.brainyquote.com/quotes/quotes/b/benjaminfr138217.html (last visited February 25, 2016).

Counsel Your Client

A successful mediation starts with client counseling. A client who has never attended mediation before will need to be educated about the mediation process. Clients should understand that mediation is an informal process with a trained and objective neutral party who will facilitate settlement discussions. The mediator is neither judge nor jury, but a facilitator. The client should be advised that while trial is about winning, mediation is about problem-solving. And the client should understand an important corollary to this: At trial, clients do not decide the outcome; the court does. In mediation, clients decide whether or not to settle, and on what terms.

Not only does mediation empower clients to resolve their dispute instead of having a resolution imposed on them, but mediation is also an opportunity to explore solutions that the law would not provide. This is an important aspect to settlement. Consensual resolution (whether through negotiation or mediation) invites creativity involved in fashioning the remedy. As a result, attorneys should spend time with clients—*before* the mediation itself—exploring approaches to resolution that arise from their business circumstances, not from the law. This requires attorneys and clients to discuss and examine the strengths and weaknesses of the legal case, but also to explore the client's underlying business concerns, opportunities, and challenges.

Recognize Cognitive Barriers

We are all human. Thus, our ability to objectively evaluate settlement offers may be clouded by innate, unavoidable cognitive barriers. Recognizing these cognitive barriers enables us to move past our blind spots to enhance settlement opportunities in mediation.

Cognitive barriers may impair accurate assessment of our own and/or the other side's legal positions, inherent risks, or factual contentions. Cognitive barriers can also impact our ability to evaluate the value of our or our adversary's legal case or the costs involved in obtaining that outcome. Unless recognized, each of these barriers can impede the mediation and settlement process.

Common cognitive barriers include the following:

a.   <u>Advocacy Bias</u>: Both client and counsel may develop advocacy bias as the case progresses. Inherently, to build a case, we must focus on the facts and law that support our position. However, over time, we become so enmeshed in our "winning" position that we may be unable to comprehend or accurately weigh the importance of adverse information. Instead, we are biased to either dismiss unfavorable information or reinterpret it to be favorable. In mediation, parties must set aside their advocacy bias and objectively examine the strengths and weaknesses of all parties to accurately evaluate settlement offers.

b.   <u>Cognitive Dissonance</u>: Cognitive dissonance is the psychological inability to consider data that contradicts our viewpoint. Instead of analyzing the nonconforming information and reevaluating the strengths and weaknesses of our case, we lash out at the other side, blaming them or devaluing their positions or interests to strengthen ours. The result is that our emotions impede the settlement process.

c.   <u>Loss Aversion</u>: Loss aversion is a psychological distortion causing us to negatively view any settlement proposals that we perceive to represent a loss. This response results in the rejection of offers that, if re-framed to sound like either a win for us or a neutral outcome, would have been accepted. For example, most clients would prefer a sure gain of $240 over a 25% likelihood of a gain of $1,000, even though the latter choice is rationally more valuable.

d.   <u>Competitive Arousal</u>: This barrier is exactly what it sounds like. A party in mediation becomes so fixated on "winning" the negotiation (aroused by the competition) that they reject compelling settlement offers because of their need to feel they have defeated their opponent and obtained a better settlement than would otherwise have been achieved.

When preparing for mediation and during the mediation, parties (*both* clients *and* counsel) should make every effort to overcome cognitive barriers and be prepared to consider settlement parameters and settlement offers on the basis of their merit.

Analyze Your BATNA and WATNA

To meaningfully consider a settlement offer, parties must analyze the consequences of rejecting the offer and cratering the negotiation. This requires parties to consider their BATNA and WATNA. This analysis should begin prior to mediation and be reassessed throughout the course of the mediation. Knowing your BATNA and WATNA will provide you with a basis to evaluate offers made during the mediation.

Determining your BATNA and WATNA requires a multifaceted analysis. It is not simply "what do I get if I win" versus "what do I get if I lose." Instead, it takes into consideration all of the costs associated with winning or losing. Factors to be considered include quantifiable costs of going to trial (i.e., attorney's fees, expert fees, court costs, etc.), intangible costs of going to trial (lost productivity, reputation concerns and publicity, witness availability, etc.), likelihood of success on the merits, and collectability of any judgment. Other variables to consider are the time value of money, the risk that there will be new developments in the law that help or hurt your position, potential precedential value of any adverse ruling by the court, and any desire between the parties for ongoing business relationships.

For illustrative purposes, assume a simple contract dispute in which Party A asserts that Party B owes it $100,000. If Party A believes that it has a 70% likelihood of success at trial and that it will cost $30,000 to try the case, then its BATNA is $49,000 (70% of $70,000), while its WATNA is –$10,000 (30% of –$30,000, which is the result arising from losing a trial and having to pay $30,000 in legal fees). Because Party A's BATNA is $49,000 while its WATNA is –$10,000, using a BATNA/WATNA analysis, Party A should accept any offer in excess of $49,000 and consider any offer more favorable than –$10,000.

It is important to thoughtfully evaluate your BATNA and WATNA prior to starting the mediation. Depending on the complexity of the dispute, this analysis may not be feasible "on the fly" at mediation. In addition, parties in mediation should constantly reexamine their BATNA/WATNA analysis during the course of the mediation. Information shared through the mediation process may impact the underlying assumptions and, thus, change the assessment of your BATNA or WATNA or both.

Consider Settlement Options in Advance

Particularly in complex matters, parties should consider settlement options prior to starting the mediation. This includes exploring their interests (rather than positions) implicated in the dispute. Interests represent the "why care" of the litigation. Why does either party care whether it wins or loses? While the dispute may nominally be about money, often there are other factors. For example, there could be underlying business concerns (e.g., competition, reputation, publicity, safety, or quality control) or financial concerns (e.g., liquidity, solvency, or covenant violations). Identifying and understanding each side's interests is often an important step towards developing a creative solution to the problem. After all, an agreement will be reached only on terms that address and satisfy the other side's concerns.

Equally important is exploring nonmonetary consideration that a party could offer or request as part of any settlement. Nonmonetary consideration includes an apology, discounts on future purchases, repair or modification of defective products, policy changes, letters of recommendation, outplacement services, or renegotiation of an existing contract. This is an area ripe for creativity. It is not uncommon that the nonmonetary components are what ultimately bridge the parties to settlement.

Educate and Use Your Mediator

A mediator is a neutral third-party responsible for the mediation process while the parties are responsible for the outcome. Because the mediator is neither party nor judge, the mediator is coming "cold" to the dispute with no prior knowledge. It is important to educate the mediator about the underlying facts, the legal theories of liability and defense, prior settlement talks, actual or perceived barriers to resolution, and business concerns and considerations.

In mediation, information is currency. The mediator needs money in the bank (i.e., to be fully informed) to effectively facilitate settlement of your dispute. With this information, the mediator can help parties gauge the timing and method of sharing information throughout the mediation process. The better informed the mediator is, the better job the mediator can do.

Mediators are there to serve. They want to help the parties reach the best possible settlement for their case, so use this incentive to your advantage. A good mediator wants you to share everything that might shed light on the case, whether it's a legal concern or not. Is there a concern for the safety of your client? Do you have a client with a difficult personality or one with unrealistic expectations? Do you have compelling facts, but bad law? Do you have compelling law, but bad facts? Do you have compelling facts and law, but there are other circumstances you perceive to be favorable to the other side? Inform your mediator about all of these items. The mediator's job is to facilitate a settlement. To be successful, the mediator must understand your strengths and your weaknesses. Moreover, state and federal laws frequently protect communications before, during and after mediation with both confidentiality and evidentiary privilege and render the mediator incompetent to offer testimony as to the content of mediation communications.

Conclusion

Whether the mediation involves pending litigation, a prelitigation dispute or a stuck business negotiation, preparation is invaluable. Know your BATNA and WATNA. Understand your business considerations. Educate your mediator. Be open to alternatives and creative solutions.

Following these suggestions may improve your chances of achieving a favorable settlement through mediation. It is also important to remember that, while the goal of mediation is consensual resolution, even if the dispute is not resolved at mediation, parties tend to leave mediation with a better understanding of their dispute, strategic considerations, and settlement options. As a result, mediation is a valuable process for litigants whether or not the matter settles.

CHAPTER 3

An ADR Glossary

EDITOR'S NOTE: As legal fields evolve, their terms multiply and change. "Alternative Dispute Resolution," or "ADR," used to mean either negotiated settlement or (in North America) arbitration. Now the term embraces a variety of processes, each with unique objectives and many with subtle distinctions. The glossary offered below may be of help in keeping track of the intentions of this Workbook's authors, as well as those of counterparties in transactional drafting and dispute resolution processes.

Adjudication

Generically, the resolution of disputes through appeal to a neutral third-party vested (by operation of law or agreement) with authority to bind the disputants to the terms of an award. Common adjudicative processes are trial and arbitration. In the United Kingdom, "Adjudication" refers to a dispute resolution process in construction contracts as set forth in the Housing Grants, Construction and Regeneration Act 1996, and the regulations promulgated thereunder (1998 No. 649).

Alternative Dispute Resolution ("ADR")

An approach to conflict resolution designed to circumvent public litigation or other adjudicative processes. In North America, ADR has taken one of two forms: Arbitration or mediation. However, the modern approach to ADR encompasses an array of hybrid systems, combining elements of arbitration and mediation. In other regions, particularly Europe, ADR often is used synonymously with mediation.

Arbitration

A voluntary adjudicative method of dispute resolution in which an independent, impartial and neutral third-party (an arbitrator or arbitral panel) considers arguments and evidence from disputing parties and then renders a decision or award. Arbitration may be binding or non-binding, with levels of procedural formality varying according to the parties' contractual agreement. Almost without exception, arbitration is a creature of contract, and both the powers of the arbitrator and the conduct of the arbitration process are determined by the parties at the time of their agreement to arbitrate. In the absence of an agreement to the contrary, arbitral awards cannot be judicially appealed except on very limited statutory grounds.

Arb/Med

A hybrid process (see below) by which an arbitrator is asked to serve as mediator to assist the parties in resolving the dispute at hand prior to issuance of the award. To ensure the integrity of the arbitration process while at the same time giving full rein to the mediator's skills, the practice is usually observed at the end of the arbitration hearing and after the award has been drafted, but prior to its issuance. The parties are thus assured that in the event that the arbitrator's efforts to mediate a resolution are unsuccessful, the ultimate award has not been tainted by any knowledge the arbitrator may have gained on an *ex parte* basis during the mediation.

Baseball Arbitration

In this arbitral process, each party submits a proposed monetary award to the arbitrator. At the conclusion of the hearing, the arbitrator is required to select one of the two proposed awards without modification. This requirement (sometimes called "Last Offer Arbitration" or LOA) severely limits the arbitrator's discretion because it yields one of two outcomes, neither of which might be the "right" one. A common consequence of Baseball Arbitration is to give the parties an incentive to conduct their negotiations diligently and to submit to the arbitrator a reasonable proposal, in the hope that it will be adopted. In a related variation, "Night Baseball Arbitration," the parties agree privately to conform the arbitrator's award to the last offer that is closest to it. Thus, the arbitrator is unaware of the parties' intention and renders an award based on the merits without restriction, which the parties then privately convert to an award that conforms to their agreement.

Bounded Arbitration

In this variant of arbitration, the parties agree privately (without informing the arbitrator) that the arbitrator's final award will be adjusted to a bounded range that the parties have agreed upon. It is used to manage the risk of an unanticipated, unwelcome outcome. Thus, if the respondent is willing to pay $60,000 and the claimant is willing to accept $100,000, their Bounded Arbitration agreement would provide that (1) if the arbitrator awards an amount below $60,000, the award will be conformed to $60,000; (2) if the award exceeds $100,000, the award will be reduced to $100,000; and (3) if the award is within the range, the parties are bound by the figure in the award. Alternatively, limits to the arbitrator's award may be expressed in the agreement to arbitrate, and the arbitrator is therefore required to make an award that falls between the two bounds set forth.

Confidential Listening

A quick "screening" process in which the parties each privately informs a neutral third-party their confidential settlement positions, and the third-party informs them whether they are within settlement range.

Court-Annexed ADR

Alternative dispute resolution administered by or otherwise institutionally affiliated with a court. Some courts require or urge disputants to participate in various ADR processes at various points in the litigation, including judicial settlement conference, mediation, early neutral evaluation, and summary jury trial. Some courts directly offer such services; others maintain a list of approved providers of such services who are not themselves formally affiliated with the court administration.

Delegation

In arbitration, a provision in an agreement to arbitrate that determines who will decide the validity of that agreement. In the absence of clear, unmistakable evidence that the parties agreed to delegate that responsibility to an arbitrator, a court is charged with determining the existence and validity of an arbitration agreement.[1]

Dispute Resolution Board

A party-appointed panel chaired by a trained Neutral (see below), which generally is formed at the start of a construction project and meets regularly (usually at the site) to monitor work progress and to provide guidance to the parties. Once the DRB is in place, is informed about the project, and follows its progress, it is able to guide the parties to a mutual resolution of differences before they become disputes. In the event that the DRB is called upon to hear a ripened dispute, it can make either recommendations, awards that are binding for a period of time, awards that are binding but appealable, or final and binding decisions, depending on the agreement of the parties involved in the project. DRBs have been successfully used in complex construction projects.

---

1. First Options of Chicago, Inc. v. Kaplan, 514 U.S. 938 (1995).

Dispute Management Systems Design

A formal, institutionalized method for managing streams of conflicts within an enterprise. The term refers to managerial systems established in corporations or similar entities that experience disputes and conflicts within the organization (such as employment or executive compensation disputes) or between the organization and its external business relationships (such as with governments, consumers, regulatory agencies, competitors, and vendors). Many Dispute Management Systems involve the use of an Ombudsman (see below). The goal of Dispute Management Systems Design is to establish a reliable, uniform policy by which efficient, fair and commercially rational methods are devised to identify, assess, and manage corporate risk from disputes.[2]

Early Neutral Evaluation

Often used in Court-Annexed ADR (see above), Early Neutral Evaluation provides disputants with a frank professional evaluation of their claims and defenses by a professional, objective observer—often a Magistrate Judge. It is often particularly helpful when the parties disagree significantly about the value of their cases and are locked in positional bargaining. ENE benefits the parties by adding to the negotiation certain assessments whose neutrality may lend them authority and utility without changing their positions or interests.

Hybrid Process

This term refers to any ADR process that incorporates elements from different processes into a unified proceeding. An example is Arb/Med (see above).

---

2. For a reliable introduction to this topic, *see* CATHY A. COSTANTINO & CHRISTINA SICKLES MERCHANT, DESIGNING CONFLICT MANAGEMENT SYSTEMS (1996).

Impartiality

An attribute of an effective Neutral. Impartiality refers to the subjective attitude of a Neutral, who should not favor one disputant over another.

Independence

An attribute of an effective Neutral. Independence refers to the absence of any objective link (personal or business relationship) between a Neutral and any of the disputants.

Litigation

An adversarial proceeding in public court to determine and enforce legally cognizable rights and defenses. Litigation results in a judgment that awards a remedy in conformance with statutory or common law. With few exceptions, judgments resulting from litigation are appealable on a variety of legally cognizable grounds.

Mediation

Mediation is facilitated negotiation, whose object is the consensual resolution of a dispute on terms that the parties themselves agree upon. It is a form of alternative dispute resolution in which a neutral party (a mediator) selected by the parties seeks to determine the interests of the parties, discover which of these interests may be shared, and alert them to a resolution that may further those interests. At times the mediator draws the parties towards a mutually satisfactory way to "split the pie"; at other times the mediator assists the parties to invent ways to "make the pie bigger" before splitting it. Communications during mediation may be *ex parte* and are always strictly confidential and, to the extent provided by law, inadmissible as settlement negotiations. If competent to do so, and if requested by both parties, the mediator may eventually (1) offer an opinion on the parties' likelihood of success in an adjudicated proceeding, and/or (2) offer a proposed "best resolution" that the mediator considers is the fairest, most commercially rational outcome to the dispute. However, the mediator has no authority to impose an outcome on the parties and controls only the process of the mediation itself, not its result.

Med/Arb

A hybrid process (see above) pursuant to which, by agreement, the parties engage in mediation with the intention of submitting all unresolved issues to final and binding arbitration. Many commentators caution that to ensure the integrity of the arbitration process, Med/Arb agreements should provide that the arbitrator shall not be the same person who served as mediator in the matter. Other practitioners, including those in Europe and Asia, have less hesitation to engage in Med/Arb.

Mini-Trial

A hybrid process (see above) by which the parties present their legal and factual contentions to a panel of representatives selected by each party or to a neutral third-party or both. The presentations are strictly limited and, at the end of the presentations, the party representatives and/or Neutral meet and confer. The utility of the process is to provide senior party representatives with an opportunity to balance the strength of their client's claims against the contentions of their adversary, with an eye to resolving the matter on commercial rather than legal terms.

Multi-Step Clauses

Increasingly, sophisticated commercial contracts feature Multi-Step Clauses, which provide for multiple layers of dispute management. Multi-Step Clauses encourage business managers to engage in commercially rational processes prior to or in addition to legal resort. For example, a clause may call for parties to engage in good-faith notice and negotiation as a condition precedent to initiating arbitration or litigation. Some clauses require the participation of indemnitors at an early stage. Some negotiation "steps" are further divided, to contemplate the involvement of senior managers in the event that junior managers could not resolve the problem (thus rewarding junior managerial negotiation skills and often removing from the negotiation process the individual whose conduct is at issue). Mediation is frequently called for, either prior to initiation of a formal claim or at a designated point in the prosecution of such a claim. Some Multi-Step Clauses also set forth a schedule for the exchange of certain information, so that mediation can take place early in the process in an informed manner. In the event of failure to resolve the dispute in these methods, the clauses call for arbitration or litigation, usually also addressing the parties' selection of venue, choice of law, waiver of jury, and other issues. Ideally, a Multi-Step Clause identifies the benefit that the parties seek to derive from the deal that the contract documents and devises a means for the parties to protect that intended benefit to the maximum degree possible.

Negotiation

A method of exchanging interests and proposals through direct communication. Many ADR practitioners distinguish "Positional" and "Interest-based" negotiation. The former is driven by the assessment of desired outcomes and the iterative exchange of those outcomes towards a compromise. The latter is informed by the parties' ultimate commercial objectives and the exchange of proposals for obtaining those objectives in the context of the other parties' interests.

Neutral

A third-party (arbitrator or mediator) who interposes in a dispute with the extent of authority granted by the parties (except in the case of a judge, whose authority is granted by law). Internationally promulgated ethical standards require that Neutrals shall exhibit Independence, Impartiality and Neutrality (see individual terms).

Neutrality

An attribute of an effective Neutral. Neutrality refers to the Neutral's having no personal or institutional interest in the outcome of a dispute.

Ombudsman

A third-party who deals with conflicts on a confidential basis and gives disputants information on how to resolve the problem at issue. In the United States, institutional Ombudsman offices are created by some corporations to provide resources for employees, "whistle blowers," consumers and others. In Europe, the Ombudsman's role has traditionally involved the management of complaints by the public against public administrative agencies.

Settlement Counsel

Settlement Counsel is a party representative who is marginally involved, or sometimes strictly uninvolved, in the prosecution of claims or defenses in the course of an adjudicative process but instead is responsible for the resolution of the dispute at the earliest possible time on the best possible terms. Some law firms offer clients the option to engage both "trial counsel" and "settlement counsel" in an effort to create conditions that hasten optimal resolution of a dispute.

Severability

In arbitration, the legal doctrine that an agreement to arbitrate that appears as part of a larger commercial agreement is considered severable from the rest of the contract for purposes of enforceability. The doctrine of severability means that a challenge to the contract as a whole does not constitute a challenge to the enforceability of the agreement that the parties made to arbitrate such claims.[3]

---

3. *See* Prima Paint Corp. v. Flood & Conklin Mfg. Co., 388 U.S. 395 (1967).

CHAPTER 4

Considerations in Negotiating and Drafting Dispute Management Clauses in Commercial Contracts

F. Peter Phillips[1]

EDITOR'S NOTE: Much of the benefit of avoiding litigation is anticipating possible sources of conflict at the inception of the deal and devising commercially rational mechanisms to identify and deal with disputes before they ripen. This chapter offers guidance to attorneys charged with papering commercial deals, with an eye to using dispute management clauses to preserve the value of the deal and allocate risk.

Few commercial transactions are executed without a hitch, and the foresighted business manager will seek to anticipate those contingencies. Alternative Dispute Resolution, if well managed, can be an attractive alternative to traditional litigation in addressing disputes arising from business transactions. Where else but in the deal documents can parties choose, well in advance or at the time the dispute arises, the applicable law, procedure, rules, language, service provider, scope of discovery, venue, timing, and ultimately the neutral(s) who will expeditiously, privately and confidentially hear and decide the matter?

---

1. This chapter is based on DRAFTING DISPUTE MANAGEMENT CLAUSES: A PRACTICAL GUIDE FOR THE TRANSACTIONAL LAWYER, a publication of the ABA Section on Business Law (2010) (co-authored with Terry L. Trantina and appearing here by permission).

Clients often voice dissatisfaction with the quality, cost, delay, and unreliability of commercial dispute resolution processes. Their professional advisors are increasingly expected to anticipate and avoid these problems. An important place to do that is in the contract at the time of the deal.

No contract drafter can foresee every change on the ground or every good-faith interpretive disagreement that will occur over the term of the deal. The drafters' challenge, therefore, is to devise processes for the economic management and efficient resolution of unknown and unknowable contingencies.

This chapter is intended as a resource for transactional attorneys seeking to ensure that dispute resolution clauses in the contracts they draft meet the reasonable commercial expectations of their clients and add value to the deal.[2]

Why Not Just Sue?

Most businesses aren't eager to take a business dispute to court, particularly if they have been there before. It is extremely wasteful of their time, energy, and money, and poses outcome risks that they can't always manage or accurately assess. The litigation process is commercially irrational. It also exposes business problems to the public and allows strangers and even competitors to rummage through the client's file drawers. It is layered with time-consuming, unfathomable, often unjustifiable, costly, and repeated delays. The outcome is unpredictable and dependent on principles of general application and people who are not aware of or competent in the business plans of the parties or their market.

Perhaps the most irritating aspect of the business litigation process is that businessmen and businesswomen must give up control to others—e.g., their own lawyers, the opposing parties' lawyers, court clerks, judges and nameless members of juries—to move the process forward and to produce outcomes affecting their businesses, perhaps in material ways. Litigation appears to the business client to be out of control, chewing up resources and forestalling other opportunities,

---

2. This chapter concerns only domestic deals and only business-to-business contracts. Cross-border transactions and employment or consumer disputes raise very different issues that this chapter does not attempt to address.

yet having little likelihood of an outcome that will make all the aggravation and effort worthwhile. There is seldom a return on a litigation investment.

What Are the Options?

Commercial dispute resolution processes can be divided into two categories—processes in which the parties *retain* control over the procedure and the outcome, and processes in which they *cede* that control. The first category includes consensual processes, such as negotiation, facilitated negotiation, mediation, early neutral evaluation, joint expert evaluation, and summary or advisory mini-trial. The second category includes two adjudicative processes: Private (arbitration) and public (trial).

When presented in those terms, most commercial enterprises prefer consensual processes. They yield more commercially rational results, are within the control of the disputants (in terms of cost, duration, and outcomes), are confidential, and are driven by business rather than legal concerns. The transaction costs for consensual processes tend to be lower than adjudicative processes by orders of magnitude. The business disputants can decide how long the process will last, how much it will cost, how it will be conducted, and—most critically—the attributes of the decision concluding the dispute. It is therefore almost always advisable to frame contractual dispute resolution clauses in deal documents in a manner so as to exhaust consensual processes before incurring the multiple disadvantages of adjudicative methods of dispute resolution.

This strategy yields a structured contract provision called a "stepped" or "tiered" contract clause—direct negotiation that leads, in the event of an impasse, to mediation (or other consensual ADR methods) and, only in the event of failure of these processes to produce an agreed-upon result, to arbitration or litigation.

Isn't ADR Kind of "Touchy-Feely"?

ADR is a management tool used to manage the kind of risk that is presented by disputes arising from a deal. ADR law is neither recondite nor impenetrable, and the procedural issues that arise in the course of mediation and arbitration tend to be both identifiable and manageable.

ADR law is straightforward. Many states have adopted the Uniform Mediation Act or some variant of it, and many more courts have adopted rules addressing mediation. A body of case law, almost all of it state-specific, has been developed to determine such threshold issues as the enforceability of a contractual obligation to mediate or negotiate, what constitutes "good faith," the limits and enforceability of mediation confidentiality (including whether statements made during mediation are admissible as evidence), the enforceability of agreements arising from mediation, the competence of a mediator to give testimony in subsequent related court proceedings, and so on.

Arbitration law is even more richly established, though perhaps somewhat more abstruse. Simply put, the Federal Arbitration Act (FAA)[3] provides that federal courts may compel parties to arbitrate if they have agreed to do so, and may enforce and convert to judgments arbitration awards. They may also issue orders vacating arbitration awards, under very narrow guidelines.[4] States have enacted arbitration laws that, in essence, conform to the FAA. The FAA is applicable to all transactions "involving interstate commerce," a standard that reaches the limits of the Constitution's Commerce Clause power.

Therefore, to the continuing surprise of many lawyers, most commercial contracts are governed by the FAA, not state arbitration law, whether the contract mentions the FAA or not and even if the contract contains a general "boilerplate" choice of law clause that expressly identifies a specific state's law as governing the contract. Note, however, that the FAA has no effect on federal *jurisdiction*. A party seeking to enter federal court to compel arbitration or to affirm or vacate an arbitration award must plead an independent basis for personal and subject matter jurisdiction. In the alternative, the claimant must seek relief in an appropriate state court pursuant to that state's arbitration act.

---

3. 9 U.S.C. §§ 1-16 (West, Westlaw through Pub. L. 114-114 (excluding 114-94, 114-95, and 114-113) approved 12-28-2015) 344.

4. Section 10(a) of the FAA provides in part that a court "may make an order vacating the award upon the application of any party to the arbitration–

    (1)   Where the award was procured by corruption, fraud, or undue means.

    (2)   Where there was evident partiality or corruption in the arbitrators, or either of them.

    (3)   Where the arbitrators were guilty of misconduct in refusing to postpone the hearing, upon sufficient cause shown, or in refusing to hear evidence pertinent and material to the controversy; or of any other misbehavior by which the rights of any party have been prejudiced, or

    (4)   Where the arbitrators exceeded their powers, or so imperfectly executed them that a mutual, final, and definite award upon the subject matter submitted was not made."

As interpreted by the U.S. Supreme Court, the FAA allows the drafter of a pre-dispute arbitration provision to dictate nearly every aspect of the dispute resolution process[5] and to have that provision enforced by both state and federal courts precisely as written. Furthermore, the FAA preempts any inconsistent provision of any state law that is not of general applicability or is directed to arbitration of disputes, as well as any that would interfere with enforcement of the arbitration obligation as long as the provision is not unconscionable—i.e., as long as the arbitration process set forth in the agreement is substantively and procedurally fair. Procedural fairness prohibits any process that would give advantage to one party or deprive a party of a timely, merit-based inquiry. The requirement of procedural fairness does not restrict process design, only unconscionable abuse.

How Do I Start Thinking About the Dispute Resolution Clause?

Conflict resolution processes that are embedded in the initial agreement should be designed to **protect the value of the deal** in the event of breach or dispute. The analysis should be straightforward: Identify the core value that the client seeks from the venture, assume a risk of nonperformance from some unidentified cause, and devise methods to manage that eventuality that are designed to preserve, to the extent possible, that value.

First, take some time to **understand the client's business needs**, i.e., the nature of likely (or less likely, but significant) disputes; the nature of the business relationships or changing circumstances that may cause these disputes; what the client most seeks to avoid in resolving disputes in court; and what, in affirmative terms, will be required—in a process, or the background of the neutral, or in cost or time concerns—to produce a merits-based resolution consistent with the client's business expectations.

Second, **become familiar with the state and federal case law** that has identified flaws in other ADR clauses in commercial contracts. The basic principle flowing through all of the law is that ADR provisions

---

5. One exception is that the parties may not, by contract, amend the FAA's provisions concerning the standards for judicial enforcement or vacatur of an arbitrator's award, as set forth in Section 10 of the FAA.

are to be given effect and enforced precisely as the parties expressly provide in their agreement. There are a number of instances in which the court observes that "if the clause had only expressly provided for [X], the court would have had no choice but to enforce it," but because the ADR clause was vague or silent on the issue, the court could not grant the party's post-dispute request for relief from the effects of the boilerplate arbitration clause. The lesson is if you want it, you had better negotiate for it.

Third, ***don't mindlessly copy another ADR clause*** that was custom-designed for another client and another deal. That kind of drafting actually may be worse than using the boilerplate clause or having no clause at all.

Fourth, ***use an up-to-date issues checklist*** when drafting ADR clauses. Each time you run across another court decision that addresses a flaw in someone else's ADR clause or adds a new gloss on an old issue, modify your checklist.

In practice, this might involve such questions as these: Should the counterparty be required to continue performance during a dispute? May payment be suspended or placed in escrow during the pendency of claimed nonperformance? Should judicial access be agreed upon (or waived) for immediate preliminary relief, such as attachment or injunction? Would the client better avail itself of legal precedent (trial) or commercial rationality (arbitration)? Is the counterparty critical to other areas of the client's business, so that the overall relationship is more important than waging war over this particular aspect of this particular deal? Should "buffers" be built in to make it difficult for the counterparty to abruptly terminate performance? Does the counterparty have assets in the client's home jurisdiction that may be subject to attachment?

A straightforward checklist is offered in the section below. Drafters should develop their own, as experience dictates.

A Suggested Checklist

The drafter seeking to preserve the value of the deal must be familiar with the rudimentary concerns of dispute risk management. These are the fundamental questions that each drafter should pose to determine whether the draft dispute resolution clause is fit for the task, whether the specific agreement is responsive to the parties' specific expectations in terms of the time and expense of resolving the problem, and whether the risks of breach are appropriately allocated.

- **Notice:** To whom should notice of a dispute be given to trigger the process? How soon after the event giving rise to the dispute must notice be given? What specificity should the notice contain?
- **Scope:** Are all matters to be treated the same way, or are certain sensitive matters (such as alleged breaches of confidentiality or misuse of intellectual property) to be carved out of the scope of the clause and subject to immediate judicial relief?
- **Rules and Initiation:** How are formal processes such as mediation or arbitration formally initiated, and what procedural rules will be followed?
- **Administered or Unadministered:** Shall the formal processes be administered by an ADR provider body (such as JAMS or AAA Rules contemplate) or will the parties choose rules that contemplate direct commencement of the process and its administration by the appointed neutral rather than by the provider organization (such as CPR Non-Administered Rules contemplate)?
- **Time Periods:** To ensure efficiency and commercial good faith, shall the various steps of the process be limited? For example, shall mediation commence automatically, regardless of the status of direct negotiations, if the dispute persists after XX days from notice?
- **Designated Representatives:** Shall the parties designate in the contract the level and seniority of their negotiators? What happens if that person is not available and willing to serve? Should the negotiation stage continue at a higher level if the initial negotiators are unsuccessful after a certain period of time?
- **Location:** Shall the mediation or arbitration occur at the location of one party or in a third place? (This provision can be used in bargaining to persuade a skeptical counterparty to agree to inclusion of a pre-dispute provision, especially in circumstances of unequal resources such as franchise disputes.)
- **Information Exchange:** Shall initial notice of a dispute be accompanied by documents and information sufficient to advise

the receiving party of the facts giving rise to the claim? Shall the factual basis of defenses be promptly exchanged as well? In arbitration, shall costly discovery processes, such as electronic communications, interrogatories and depositions, be limited to prevent small disputes from posing large expenses?

- **Privilege and Confidentiality:** Are the various ADR processes to remain confidential? Are statements and information exchanged in the course of settlement discussions inadmissible in a subsequent or parallel proceeding?
- **Conditions Precedent:** Must negotiations take place prior to mediation, and must mediation take place prior to initiating arbitration or litigation? Are there any exceptions?
- **Tolling:** Shall the statute of limitations with respect to adjudicative processes be tolled during the course of consensual ADR processes?
- **Provisional and Interim Relief:** May the parties seek immediate provisional relief from a court or an arbitrator? If so, with respect to what relief, and to what end?
- **Continuing Performance and Right of Termination:** Are the parties to continue to perform during the pendency of the dispute? Do the ADR provisions have the practical effect of undermining any party's termination rights?
- **Selection of the Neutral:** Shall the mediator or arbitrator be selected pursuant to institutional rules, or shall the parties do so themselves? Whether selected through an institution or directly, do the parties wish to include in the contract certain criteria to guide the selection (i.e., XX years in private practice, former government official, YY years in procurement, etc.)? If the parties choose to handle the selection of the neutral themselves, how shall that selection process be structured? Do the parties want to have a single arbitrator or a multiple-arbitrator panel, and if the latter, do they want party-appointed arbitrators to be neutral?
- **Awards, Costs and Fees:** How shall the costs of the mediation or arbitration be allocated? Is an arbitral tribunal free to make any award it wishes, or shall its powers be bounded in some way? May punitive or consequential damages be awarded? May the tribunal award attorney fees or neutral fees to the prevailing party?

- **Form of Award:** Shall the arbitral award be reasoned (written)? Shall the tribunal be required to issue its award within a specified period of time after close of the hearing?
- **Customized ADR Processes and Other Issues:** Parties may wish to create an ADR process that suits their precise needs. For example, shall they jointly engage a single expert to opine on (or even to decide) technological or other issues that are in dispute? Shall the arbitrator offer to mediate the matter after drafting the award but before issuing it? Shall the arbitration take place in a specified language and if so, who pays for the translation? What law shall govern (a) the substance of the contract, (b) the arbitration process, and (c) the enforcement of the arbitration award?

Conclusion

From a managerial perspective, commercial contract disputes are unidentifiable but anticipatable contingencies. They are best viewed not as affronts or interruptions, but rather as periodic events that, if handled skillfully, will yield improvements in a contractual relationship that has proved flawed.

Business disputes can be managed and their risk controlled just as other business contingencies can be managed: Through foresight, attention, and sophisticated techniques of negotiation and risk allocation.

PART 2

Practice

CHAPTER 5

ADR in the Workplace: Managing Retention and Termination of Employees

Hugh Christie and Joseph Semo

EDITOR'S NOTE: Perhaps no area of ADR has found earlier and more consistent application than the identification, management, and resolution of disputes in the workplace. ADR literature abounds with analysis, advice, proscriptions, and war stories of employment mediation and arbitration. Here, two experts give a helpful introduction to this constantly changing area of dispute anticipation and management.

The use of Alternative Dispute Resolution procedures in the United States is well established in the labor and employment arena for unionized workers and, increasingly, in nonunionized employment. In the unionized sector where collective bargaining contracts often provide for grievance hearings, mediation, and arbitration to address workplace issues, ADR provides employees with a right to challenge work assignments and disciplinary actions, including the opportunity to dispute termination, through a process that includes an opportunity to revisit the decision with the employer, the right to representation, the ability to confront the allegations and basis for the challenged action, and the right to seek redress through (generally binding) arbitration.

The process is less well-defined in other employment contexts where the parties are not bound by a collective bargaining agreement but where dispute resolution steps might be set forth in either an employment agreement or employer policy handbook. However, stemming from discussions dating back to the 1990s, there is increased appreciation of the importance of ADR that incorporates fundamental fairness principles.[1] These principles were collected in the work of the Due Process Task Force, a group assembled from representatives of the American Arbitration Association ("AAA"), American Bar Association, American Civil Liberties Union, Federal Mediation and Conciliation Service, National Academy of Arbitrators, National Employment Lawyers Association and Society of Professionals in Dispute Resolution.[2] The Due Process Protocols (the "Protocol") are now embedded in the AAA *Employment Arbitration Rules and Mediation Procedures*. As a policy matter, the AAA will not administer a case under that program unless it determines that the process specified by the parties does not substantially and materially deviates from the minimum standards of the Protocol.

While ADR is accepted in the United States, such practices are not accepted universally and in some jurisdictions are forbidden. In other jurisdictions arbitration clauses cannot divest courts of ultimate jurisdiction.[3] Nonetheless, court-mandated ADR, both judicial and non-judicial has had particular success in achieving settlements when applied to employment disputes. Employers, however, should consult with local counsel regarding the efficiency of ADR in a particular foreign jurisdiction, not only as a result of different rules of procedures but also due to cultural differences in their jurisdiction.

Legal Framework Enabling ADR

While some courts continue to be reluctant to surrender jurisdiction to arbitration proceedings, Congress has embraced arbitration as an

---

1. For a history of the development of the Due Process Protocol *see The Due Process Protocol: Getting There and Getting Over It*, Arnold Zack, Nov. 2, 2007, http://www.law.harvard.edu/ programs/lwp/people/staffPapers/zack/Protocol%20getting%20there%20and%20over%20it.%20 PUblished%20format.pdf (last accessed February 25, 2016).

2. Renamed, Association for Conflict Resolution. For a history of the evolution of this organization, *see* http://www.imis100us2.com/ACR/ACR/About_ACR/About_US.aspx?WebsiteKey=a9a587d8-a6a4-4819-9752-ef5d3656db55&hkey=c52a2d0d-d1c3-4279-a03a-b4b98db0ffe4&New_Conte ntCollectionOrganizerCommon=3#New_ContentCollectionOrganizerCommon (last accessed February 25, 2016).

3. For a discussion of practices internationally, *see* Proskauer, International Trends in Employment Dispute Resolution: Counsel's Perspectives, (presented at World of Work: Employment Dispute Resolution Systems Across the Globe, hosted by St. John's University School of Law and Fitzwilliam College, Cambridge University, 2011), http://www.proskauer.com/files/ News/4a13f735-d2ee-4954-a18c-1b413ef25cbc/Presentation/NewsAttachment/b8ae0006-6826-4d0a-89ed-2294878f5553/Proskauer%20Worlds%20of%20Work%20Symposium%207.21.11.pdf (last visited February 25, 2016).

alternative to court litigation and made it a national policy.[4] The Supreme Court has recognized this policy and over a long period of time has continued to underscore the federal policy to encourage the voluntary settlement of disputes through arbitration.[5]

These are the leading cases in the evolution of acknowledged support for the Congressional policy:

> *Gilmer v. Interstate/Johnson Lane Corp*[6]: Finding arbitration appropriate for deciding statutory claims and noting that the Federal Arbitration Act protects against bias, by providing that courts may overturn arbitration decisions where there was evident partiality or corruption in the arbitrators.
> *Circuit City Stores, Inc. v. Adams*[7]: Finding the limitation of the FAA was limited to works in the transportation industry.
> *American Express Co. v. Italian Colors Restaurant*[8]: Finding contractual waiver of class-based action in arbitration enforceable, even in claims brought under the Sherman Act alleging antitrust violations.

The Expected Cost Efficiencies of ADR

Our system of resolving employment through litigation is widely viewed as broken. In the best of cases, both the employer and the employee feel victimized by the process and the expense, particularly the expense of counsel that can far exceed the amount in dispute. Moreover, there is always the concern that a plaintiff's counsel will feel compelled to throw in every possible claim on a "see what sticks" approach. Courts are loath to find a claim so frivolous as to justify sanctions on the party or counsel asserting such claims. While other jurisdictions' systems of litigation—those outside the United States—

---

4. Parties seeking to compel the use of ADR can face state court reluctance to deprive a litigant of his day in court. Agreements to arbitrate have been successfully challenged where, for example, an employer is found to control the process and the rules. *See, e.g.*, Bowers v. Asbury St. Louis Lex, LLC, (Mo. St. App. July 7, 2015), https://www.courts.mo.gov/file.jsp?id=88017 (last accessed February 25, 2016).

5. In AT&T Mobility LLC v. Concepcion, 131 S. Ct. 1740, (2013), the Court noted a "liberal federal policy favoring arbitration" and found that a party can be found to consent to arbitration even in a contract of adhesion.

6. 111 S. Ct. 1647 (1991).

7. 121 S. Ct. 1302 (2001).

8. 133 S. Ct. 2304 (2013).

may be "less broken," concerns about delay and disproportionate cost appear universal. In some jurisdictions, legislatures or Parliaments have established statutory tribunals to divert employment cases from the regular court system.

In all settings, a well-thought-out ADR scheme provides a mechanism to make the best out of a situation that neither party wanted to encounter. The Protocol offers guidance in establishing such a mechanism.

Making ADR Work

A designer of employment dispute systems is well advised to consider certain issues in ensuring both fairness and efficiency in addressing the use of ADR in the workplace.

Identify circumstances in which employees want or need an opportunity to have a voice in an employment-related matter.

The first step for an effective ADR program that maximizes the return to the employer and earns the trust of employees is to open a channel for communication. This suggestion is not made in derogation of the importance of a manager's open-door policy. Conversation between employee and manager will always be the beginning point of the relationship between employee and the employer. Experience, however, documents that employees will have an understandable reluctance to share all their concerns with their immediate manager who may be the source of the concern or who may then view (and judge) the employee as a "complainer." An employer will benefit from providing a channel to learn what is happening, avoiding the "if I had only known that" moment. To earn the employee's trust, and the trust of first-line management, the first-step stop for ADR is to have a point of contact charged with a responsibility to maintain discretion and confidence, a position sometimes referred to as the "ombudsman." This may be the Human Resource department. The contact must invite trust and honor any undertaking with the employee or manager who seeks to share his or her concern. This responsibility cannot be incidental but must be a recognized and published responsibility. This person should only initiate next steps, with buy-in from the person(s) who approached him or her. To state the obvious, an ombudsman position must be supported by senior management, and have sufficient authority to be able to perform its designated function.

For regulated industries and those doing business with the government where there can be liability for "false claims" or "worthless services" under federal law, it may be desirable to have multiple points of contact, and there may need to be designated persons in the chain of command, often sporting the title of compliance officer or counsel. The appropriate person to designate must be matched to the nature of the employee's concern. For these kinds of concerns, use of this point of contact might be mandatory. For example, in a medical or health benefit setting, any concern relating to improper billing should be required to be reported to a person with compliance responsibilities. Such process benefits the employee who will have a sanctioned communication and benefit the employer by permitting an opportunity to correct activity that can expose it to sanctions.[9]

In some cases, the ombudsman function blends into the whistleblower protection provided by the employer.[10]

Develop and nurture an in-house procedure to address employment concerns (whether from managers or employees) early. Assess whether a peer-to-peer intervention might help.

Each level of management must endorse early intervention. All must believe that there is value in early communication. Also, the person appointed to serve as the first-step, must be aware of the work environment so that he or she might truly add value to the conversation.

Management must assess whether this process can be a matter of culture and a positive attribute of the organization, making the employer an employer-of-choice in a competitive market. Happy employees help

---

9. In the health field, HHS has endorsed the use of compliance plans designed to identify and end improper conduct. *See, e.g.*, the OIG's Compliance 101 Web page (http://oig.hhs.gov/compliance/101/).

10. Whether disclosures to an ombudsman will be deemed disclosure that places the employer on notice of the subject discussed will depend upon all facts and circumstances, as discussions with the ombudsman may be structured to assure that the subject matter is not communicated to the employer.

recruitment; an unhappy employee can be responsible for having talent search elsewhere. To be sure, such procedures and such a culture require a leap of faith for those schooled in a more traditional management process embedded in authority and an established hierarchy.

Consider the use of an outside resource to facilitate communication.

Commitment to ADR requires consideration of whether an outside party is needed to serve the function. Employers have a good amount of experience utilizing third parties to address employee needs. A very familiar example are the Employee Assistance Programs (EAPs) that assist employees with addictions and other abuse situations that will interfere with their work (and other interpersonal contacts). These resources are available for those commonly considered problems such as alcohol and drug abuse but are equally important to address life problems that employees encounter including spousal abuse, family grieving, marital discord, credit management, and family care.

A more complex dynamic occurs when the employer attempts to use its HR department to serve as a two-hat office. The HR specialist is offered to employees to provide career/job counseling to help the worker achieve success at the job. The second function is to help evaluate the employee for promotion or better placement within (and sometimes outside) the organization.

The larger the organization and the more competitive the environment, the greater benefit one can expect from improved communication and early resolution of concerns without an adversarial process. Most recognize that if an employer fails to address an issue when it presents itself, the amount of time and effort required to address the issue later increases exponentially, positions harden, and shared opportunity is lost.

Determine the proper role for mediation of a dispute.

Mediation, whether managed through an in-house process or utilizing an outside third-party, must provide a real opportunity to address the concerns. The process is all about respect.

The beginning step in mediation is to provide an opportunity for fact finding. Presumably, the facts, or at least the sources of material information, have already been identified either in the discussions leading to the job action or in prior conversations. But if not, this is the time to get a thorough record identified. Parties may disagree on the proper resolution of a matter, but all should have a shared record to review or, in the alternative, should acknowledge how they disagree on what happened or why. Again, circumstances are important; to bolster confidence in the process an employer is likely to have to assist the employee to identify material facts and organize the presentation of the facts so there can be discussion. An assistant may need to be provided to the employee to make this meaningful.

The mediator should be a person who will command the respect of both parties and bring objectivity to the conversation. Today, a number of organizations provide training for mediators, and the parties may examine the qualifications of a mediator. An agreed-upon mediator brings buy-in to the process. By contrast, a mediator who is appointed over an employee's objections is nearly worthless.

Reasonable expectations must be agreed upon at the outset. The parties should consider whether mediation is the final ADR step or whether it is followed by an additional pre-dispute step, either final and binding arbitration or non-binding arbitration. An employer must consider which alternative is better. It may be better to provide for non-binding arbitration as a pre-dispute process; the parties may always agree to have arbitration as final and binding. An employer might, for example, agree to provide an incentive to resolve a matter through final and binding arbitration. Whatever process is suggested, it must succeed in obtaining acceptance by the employee.

Determine the proper process for entrusting the dispute to a third-party.

Absent a well-designed process, the employer is choosing to rely upon courts to resolve disputes. A decision to use litigation as the dispute resolution process is a decision to submit the dispute to either the community at-large (called a jury) or a judge. Efforts to avoid a jury will depend upon the jurisdiction where the dispute arises. In many other jurisdictions, juries are far less common than in our system. The alternative, providing for arbitration with an arbitrator selected from a particular source, improves the likelihood that the dispute will be presented to someone more familiar with the context in which the dispute arises. A wise employer will consider the dispute resolution rules and cultures of the jurisdiction being dealt with before opting for or against arbitration. Choosing one system over another without a clear understanding of one of the systems may result in unintended results.

Experience suggests that non-binding arbitration is best suited for resolving disputes in the employment context. Unless there is employee buy-in to final and binding arbitration, the employer will ultimately lose the confidence of its employees.

Understand what post-dispute process is appropriate.

Where binding arbitration is specified to resolve a dispute, further review is generally quite limited. For proceedings subject to the Federal Arbitration Act, 9 U.S.C. §§ 9-11, the statutory limitations found in § 10(a) and § 11 are exclusive.[11] An employer will enhance the benefit of ADR as a process and as a tool for building goodwill by taking steps to make certain that the process is fully understood by its employees and their representatives.

The Organizational Value of ADR

An organization stands to gain from a well-designed ADR program in the confidence engendered among workers. Absent a program that employees can believe in, the more talented employees are more likely to search for job opportunities elsewhere. On the other hand, where employees believe that the employer's processes are basically fair, one can suffer their manager more easily, knowing that the employer has a culture that embraces improvement. This culture should carry

---

11. Hall St. Assoc. v. Mattel, Inc., 128 S. Ct. 1396 (2008). Title 9 U.S.C. § 10(a) (2000 ed., Supp. V) provides:

"(a) In any of the following cases the United States court in and for the district wherein the award was made may make an order vacating the award upon the application of any party to the arbitration—

"(1) where the award was procured by corruption, fraud, or undue means;

"(2) where there was evident partiality or corruption in the arbitrators, or either of them;

"(3) where the arbitrators were guilty of misconduct in refusing to postpone the hearing, upon sufficient cause shown, or in refusing to hear evidence pertinent and material to the controversy; or of any other misbehavior by which the rights of any party have been prejudiced; or

"(4) where the arbitrators exceeded their powers, or so imperfectly executed them that a mutual, final, and definite award upon the subject matter submitted was not made."

over to all aspects of dispute resolution reducing the likelihood that an employee will bring an action solely from the frustration that accompanies the sense of not having an opportunity to be heard.

ADR Post-Employment

Much of the above relies on and assumes that the employment relationship is ongoing. Once that relationship is severed, there is less glue holding the parties together and less impetus for a shared control of the outcome. But there still remain strong cogent reasons for utilizing ADR, particularly mediation to resolve disputes around the termination of the employment relationship. Reduced cost, quicker resolution, and a greater sense of control over the result are still powerful reasons for the ex-employer and ex-employee to engage in ADR.

When a dispute is about how much notice or pay in lieu of notice or other concept of severance or termination pay is due, ADR allows the parties to resolve the matter quickly and to get on with their lives.

Particularly in cases not concerning bad behavior, mediation in particular allows employers to augment their offers to employees with nonmonetary terms, often reducing the amounts payable, in ways a court or tribunal cannot order. A simple apology about the necessity of restructuring the workforce or the offer of a letter of reference may ease the anger of an employee and reduce his or her demands.

In sum, ADR is a tool to provide employers and employees an opportunity to reach a resolution with the possibility and probability of greater buy-in by both in the marketplace.

CHAPTER 6

ADR and Bankruptcy

Timothy R. Bow, Howard Brod Brownstein, Jerry M. Markowitz, and Scott Y. Stuart

EDITOR'S NOTE: A Bankruptcy Court is peculiarly an arena of negotiation. Indeed, many if not most, U.S. Bankruptcy Courts have promulgated discretionary or presumptive mediation programs. In this chapter, bankruptcy experts offer their observations and suggestions for protecting clients' interests through principled use of collaborative negotiation, employing the value-add of a mediator.

Bankruptcy is a unique area of the law. While most litigation involves A vs. B and results in a binary outcome—either A or B wins (in the absence of a settlement)—bankruptcy typically involves multiple stakeholders who may have different liquidation priorities under applicable state law, and the outcomes may not be binary but instead "how much" rather than "whether." It is a frequent and mutually shared goal that the assets of the business or individual debtor will not just be liquidated, which might recover relatively little for the stakeholders, but rather will continue in use or operation, possibly with its obligations reset or restructured. Bankruptcy is a clear case of social engineering. Instead of encouraging a race to the courthouse by competitive creditors seeking to exercise their respective rights and remedies under applicable state law, bankruptcy imposes a temporary suspension of creditors' rights (the "automatic stay") and initiates an orderly, structured process whereby a debtor is afforded a period of time to reorganize, restructure, sell some or all of its assets, and raise debt or equity capital, or some combination of these. The implicit justification is that society—property owners, creditors, employees, communities—will realize better economic outcomes than the free-for-all of uncontrolled litigation by creditors, each seeking maximum return to the detriment of other creditors and the debtor. Opinions may differ about whether experience bears out this justification, but for the foreseeable future, bankruptcy law is a fact of life, and the ultimate proof is whether parties avail themselves of its processes.

Perhaps appropriately, bankruptcy has its roots in courts of equity, where the tribunal may tend to apply principles of fairness as much as law, can fashion remedies that are more creative than just money damages, and presides over proceedings that are so fact-rich that successful appeals of judicial decisions are relatively rare.

Although the Bankruptcy Code[1] does not include provisions directing parties to mediation, several jurisdictions have developed programs that strongly encourage the practice. Local rules have been adopted in some jurisdictions, and others have a program of presumptive mediation. Among the jurisdictions that have adopted such procedures, the use of mediation has become quite prevalent in jurisdictions such as Delaware and New York, which have attracted the filing of "mega-cases" and have some of the most well-developed mediation procedural schemes. Some jurisdictions, such as New Jersey, have even adopted local rules that include presumptive mediation as a staple of their processes and procedures.

The Bankruptcy Code is applicable to both individuals and businesses, and mediation is in widespread use with respect to both. The comments in this chapter refer mostly to business bankruptcy; however, where there are sufficient assets involved, mediation is used widely for consumer bankruptcy as well. And as described below, mediation regarding mortgage foreclosure is an especially favored dispute resolution method.

Given the characteristics of bankruptcy, it is no surprise that mediation has become widely used in its practice and procedure. Rather than a monochrome dispute between A and B, bankruptcy may involve layers of senior and junior creditors as well as internecine disputes among them, all seeking to draw water from the same (limited) well. Furthermore, since one of the principles of bankruptcy is to treat creditors of the same class in the same way and prevent creditors from

---

1. References herein to the Bankruptcy Code refer to 11 U.S.C. §§ 101 *et seq.*

gaining an edge during the 90-day period[2] prior to the bankruptcy filing, bankruptcy law contemplates a claw-back of preferential payments from creditors that received them, which creates a multiplicity of minor controversies within the bankruptcy proceeding, all of which potentially have to be adjudicated, providing a fertile ground for consensual, rather than adjudicative, disposition of disputes.

Finally, time is usually not anyone's friend in a bankruptcy case, and therefore any proliferation of controversies or protraction of the process must be avoided. (In fact, lenders and other creditors are already displaying some impatience with bankruptcy, notwithstanding its history of increased efficiency, and evidencing a preference for state law alternatives to bankruptcy such as consensual workout, assignment for benefit of creditors, and receivership.)

Best Practices in Bankruptcy Mediation

Bankruptcy mediation has become both an important practice area and a mainstay of procedure in many jurisdictions. While some jurisdictions lag behind in the use of mediation, others see it as the best, most effective way to resolve critical issues, ranging from union contracts to complicated plan confirmation issues. Other areas where mediation has grown prevalent are in the Chapter 9 arena (which covers municipal bankruptcy), as well as mass tort litigation such as in recent cases involving the bankruptcy of Catholic archdioceses whose liabilities to victims of sexual abuse exceeded their liquid assets. Bankruptcy cases, which by definition involve financial distress, typically include the reality or threat of further deterioration of assets in the absence of swift resolution, and the initial promise of a successful reorganization can quickly evaporate into a liquidating Chapter 11 or conversion to a Chapter 7 liquidation. For this reason, parties in a bankruptcy case almost universally favor a good-faith effort at mediation rather than relying on more costly, more time-consuming, and less certain litigation.

With the rise of court-annexed or mandatory bankruptcy mediation programs, many jurisdictions have created standards for

---

2. One year for insiders. *See* Bankruptcy Code § 547.

court-approved mediators. These include sanctioned training programs,[3] the requirement that mediators initially accept *pro bono* mediation cases, and some level of experience in the area. Although lists of approved mediators are maintained by the Bankruptcy Court Clerk in several jurisdictions, parties are not limited to selecting them and can agree to choose any mediator who may be qualified, rarely with interference from the court.

Another aspect of bankruptcy mediation is the widespread use of judge mediators—sitting or retired bankruptcy judges. This has become an important part of bankruptcy mediation, especially in large, complex cases, because of the level of expertise a judge mediator can bring to the process. Although mediators in general caution the parties that the mediator is not a judge and has no authority, a judge mediator can nonetheless be more credible in his or her evaluation of a situation, and such credibility may be necessary and effective in helping the parties reach a settlement.

Relatively early in the course of any bankruptcy case involving substantial assets, the Bankruptcy Court will expect the parties to submit certain issues to mediation, and the Court's calendar will be adjusted accordingly. Bankruptcy judges are typically not shy about "recommending" mediation if the parties seem recalcitrant, and while the Court cannot compel mediation, parties are usually well advised to follow the Court's suggestion. In the absence of a settlement, little about the mediation efforts will be reported to the Court beyond the fact that the parties tried in good faith, including possibly confirming that the respective principals of the parties (i.e., authorized decision makers) attended the mediation sessions.

Virtually any issue in a bankruptcy case—from the nature (e.g., secured or unsecured) and amount of a claim, to adequate protection payments to a secured creditor, to "dividing the pie" through plan confirmation—can lend itself to mediation. One of the most prevalent uses of mediation in bankruptcy is the resolution of preference and fraudulent conveyance claims, which often may follow the principal outcome of the case, e.g., plan confirmation, sale of the assets via Bankruptcy Code § 363, etc.

---

3. For example, in 2011 the American Bankruptcy Institute (ABI) created a 40-hour Bankruptcy Mediation training program, which is a collaboration among ABI, St. John's University's Center for Bankruptcy Studies and its Hugh L. Carey Center for Dispute Resolution. *See* http://www.abi. org/events/forty-hour-bankruptcy-mediation-training (last accessed February 25, 2016).

The Use of Joint Session and Caucus in Bankruptcy Mediation

Two of the principal features of nonbankruptcy business mediation are the joint session and the caucus—the former referring to the mediator's meeting together with more than one party, and the latter to meeting with just one party. In bankruptcy cases, judicious use of the joint session and the caucus can help make mediation more effective.

In the purest of mediation environments, the joint session is commonly used at the very start of mediation. The parties are brought together (often for the first time) face-to-face and with the mediator. There is typically proper premediation planning and lying of groundwork for the mediation process, and so although a joint session in the initial stage of bankruptcy mediation might be perfunctory, it can nonetheless be critical to the ultimate success of the mediation process.

Beyond the mediator's setting forth the ground rules and the expected flow of the mediation process, the joint session is often used in nonbankruptcy mediation to allow the parties to summarize their positions. There is also a cathartic venting element whereby parties can use this session to "have their say" and assure that the other party is hearing loud and clear what they have always wanted to say face-to-face but may have not had the opportunity.

In bankruptcy mediation, one party may be more familiar than others with the bankruptcy process (especially in mega-cases, where significant preference claims may be at issue), and so the joint session offers an important and valuable opportunity to engage all parties in the process equally. This can be critical to those parties who are less familiar with the bankruptcy process, and who may feel victimized, as in preference cases, where defendants may feel that "insult is being added to injury," as they are not only suffering all or part of their claim being uncollectible, but also having to disgorge payments they may have received during the preference period. Parties who are new to how the Bankruptcy Code works may come to the process with frustrations that need to be vented for the mediation to have a chance at success.

The mediator often uses this first joint session to demonstrate that he or she is in control of the mediation process and to explain that it offers an alternative to potentially expensive, and time-consuming litigation, the outcome of which is likely uncertain, especially in a court of equity such as bankruptcy. Beyond laying out the ground rules for the mediation process and the alternative of bankruptcy litigation, the mediator has an opportunity to hear the positions of the parties in their opening statements and might offer limited feedback to them in summary form. It also allows the parties to hear each other's value propositions and critical points, as the mediator helps "set the table" for the mediation process.

The joint session gives the mediator and the parties an opportunity to "touch and feel" where everyone stands. An effective bankruptcy mediator will evaluate whether the joint session is advancing or hindering the progress of the mediation. The mediator can use this opportunity to focus the parties on what needs to be addressed going forward, and the parties can probe each other to get a feel of where things stand at that point in time, as well as what compromises might be possible. As the vast majority of bankruptcy mediations are focused on problem solving as opposed to evaluative decision making, issues can valuably get focused and narrowed during this part of the process.

In the most effective joint sessions, the mediator is more of an active listener, a technique that is particularly effective if the mediator sees the parties advancing discussion in a positive way. Still, the mediator's careful observation is critical here. The joint session can quickly become counterproductive if venting and discussion turn to anger and animosity, defeating the self-determinative and facilitative nature of the process. Active listening will also aid the bankruptcy mediator's efforts to identify each side's most important issues and interests.

For example, in bankruptcy the debtor may seek to modify prepetition collective bargaining agreements. Aside from the economic issues, a great deal of emotion may be involved when hard-won wage and work rule issues are now in jeopardy, not to mention the desire of union representatives to appear to their constituencies as effective champions for their cause.

So in a joint session, it is important that each side have its turn to speak and be clearly heard by the opposing side. Just as important, the mediator must show empathy, understanding and validation through active listening. The mediator can build confidence with the parties if they can see how the mediator reacts to each side's issues and interests with all parties present.

Caucus can be an effective tool for private discussion or to ameliorate heated emotions that may have been manifested during a joint session. The question arises, when is caucus most effective, and therefore, when is the right time to break into private sessions with each party?

Some bankruptcy mediators go right into a caucus after a brief joint session without any delay. Experience has shown that the best time for use of caucus may be when the joint session has served its purpose of letting each side have its say, when things seem to be breaking down, and/or when issues arise that are clearly sensitive or confidential and should be addressed privately.

The passage of time is usually a real factor in bankruptcy, and so proceeding directly to caucus after an initial joint session may be advantageous. Bankruptcy mediation largely involves only monetary issues, and so the parties themselves may favor proceeding to caucus directly after a joint session. Caucus in bankruptcy mediation should be used both to narrow and to focus the issues, as well as to aid the parties in assessing their own position. These can be tough discussions, but the mediator is there to facilitate, and that may include helping the parties look at aspects of their case that they have not previously addressed or have mistakenly overvalued, either outside of the mediation or during the joint session.

Caucus is a confidential process, and parties should always be reminded of this. What is discussed in a party caucus can be disclosed to another party only with the consent of the caucus party. So why utilize a caucus? Because caucus may allow "cooler heads" to prevail, and there tends to be less posturing or taking of extreme positions when the opponent is not present. Also, parties may not want to disclose certain matters to another party, at least not yet. In any case, the mediator should be mindful of why a caucus is being used and assure that it achieves its purpose. An effective mediator may prompt parties in a caucus to give themselves a "reality check" on their position and how far they can realistically expect the other party to go in compromising. The value of cultivating trust between the mediator and the parties cannot be overestimated.

Among the characteristics that distinguish bankruptcy mediation is the uniqueness of the laws that are at issue. The caucus can be an effective tool to allow the mediator to maintain control over the process, especially where the issues are complex and/or emotions may be running high. Private caucus gives both the parties and the mediator the opportunity to explore what the critical issues are that may be obstacles to settlement and how those issues might be overcome.

Many mediators employ a hybrid style, combining elements of joint session and caucus. Once a caucus has taken place, some mediators do not favor returning to a joint session until there has been movement by one or both sides in their respective positions or until a settlement may be close at hand. Those that use a hybrid style, however, often bring parties right back into joint session after a caucus as a way to highlight progress, focus upon outstanding issues, or just reaffirm that this is the parties' process and not that of the mediator. The hybrid approach may keep the process from going stale and maintain momentum, allowing the parties and the mediator a continuity of interaction. This is particularly critical in bankruptcy mediation because the fluidity of the underlying situation of the business involved may change during the mediation process.

The Role of a Financial Advisor in Bankruptcy Mediation

In Chapter 11 bankruptcy, the debtor is often assisted by a Financial Advisor (FA) or Chief Restructuring Officer (CRO), who acts in an advisory or managerial role, respectively. These advisors often take the lead in handling the bankruptcy-specific tasks, such as arranging for debtor-in-possession (DIP) financing, providing periodic reports to the Bankruptcy Court, dealing with vendors and claims, and preparing the debtor's Plan of Reorganization and Disclosure Statement.

Debtors may seek court approval of a Financial Advisor pursuant to § 327 of the Bankruptcy Code, which governs employment of professionals during a bankruptcy proceeding. Chief Restructuring Officer is an officer role addressing a host of intensive restructuring or bankruptcy-related tasks that the affected company's management team must perform, even as their full-time day jobs continue and are likely to have ramped up in terms of urgency and difficulty. These special tasks typically involve parties with which the incumbent management team has had little experience—bankruptcy courts, creditor committees, the Office of the U.S. Trustee, etc.—as well as matters that are similarly unfamiliar, such as managing for cash instead of to achieve return on investment (ROI), market share, or share price, and the court-specific duties described above. The appointment of a CRO is created through action of the company's board of directors or LLC members, consistent with its bylaws or operating agreement and applicable state corporation law, and may involve Bankruptcy Code provisions in addition to or instead of § 327.

In few such situations is time on the side of the debtor seeking to reorganize, and therefore the expense, delay, and distraction occasioned by litigation of any kind is often simply not affordable. This is one of the reasons that bankruptcy mediation has become so widespread, and those acting in the FA/CRO role typically favor an early resort to mediation regarding any disputes in the case that would otherwise get litigated.

In fact, even prepetition (i.e., before the bankruptcy filing), an FA or CRO that has been engaged to assist the company, including with preparation for a possible bankruptcy filing, will typically seek to move any pending litigation into a mode of alternative dispute resolution for the same reasons as stated above: Even if the company has a "good case," the expense, delay and distraction involved with litigation may pose too great a risk to the company's survival through the reorganization process.

And after the bankruptcy proceeding—post-confirmation of a Plan of Reorganization or following a sale of the business via Bankruptcy Code § 363—there is typically a good deal of cleanup required due to "preferences and avoidances," which are claims created by the bankruptcy proceeding that are designed to level the playing field among each class of creditors. Under the preference provisions of the Bankruptcy Code, the debtor may claw back payments made during the 90 days preceding the bankruptcy filing (or one year, in the case of an insider) that exceeded what a creditor would have otherwise received via a Chapter 7 liquidation on the filing date of the Chapter 11 proceeding.

In addition, other transactions may be avoided, and the debtor may seek disgorgement of funds received by others. Needless to say, preferences and avoidances can involve a proliferation of claims and create a substantial litigation burden on the debtor and the defendants (typically creditors) as well as the bankruptcy court. The issues in such cases are nearly all fact-based: What payments did the creditor receive and when, did the creditor change its payment terms or otherwise apply pressure during the preference period, and do the allegedly preferential payments fall within any of a handful of statutory exceptions, such as the creditor's having been paid according to the terms of its sale to the debtor and consistent with how the creditor had historically been paid, or how suppliers in that industry are typically paid. For these reasons, use of mediation in resolving preference and avoidance claims is nearly universal in bankruptcy, and there is an anecdotal but widely reported desire by bankruptcy judges that such claims be settled through mediation and not require hearings (except in unusual or very large claims).

Especially in large bankruptcy cases, these claw-back claims may constitute a significant portion of the potential litigation. In recent years, the vast majority of these claims have been sent to mediation, either on an individual case basis or through standing court orders that set up procedures for preference mediation specifying the timing and location of mediation as well as the mediator's fees.

As mediation has come into more widespread use in bankruptcy, turnaround and restructuring professionals have become very familiar with the mediation process and often participate in such mediations as the debtor's representative or as an expert in proving the historical payment practices between the debtor and a specific creditor/defendant.

Mediation in Consumer Bankruptcy Cases and Mortgage Modification Mediation in Bankruptcy

Mediation is used in a number of consumer bankruptcy contexts. It is not uncommon for a debtor and a trustee or a creditor to mediate issues central to the administration of a bankruptcy case. These may include discharge and dischargeability proceedings, actions regarding a debtor's exemption issues and turnover, and various other issues related to claims resolution.

Mortgage modification mediation is a prominent development in bankruptcy mediation that was created to address mortgage foreclosure issues brought about by the recent mortgage foreclosure crisis. Florida, one of the hardest-hit states during the recent foreclosure crisis, developed what has become a model for mortgage modification through mediation. In states where consumer bankruptcies are particularly prominent, this program has helped stay a wave of foreclosures that may have otherwise resulted.

At the start of the crisis, funds from the Troubled Asset Relief Program (TARP") were issued to some of the largest servicers of mortgages, and those services agreed to modify the home loans of borrowers. By using the mortgage modification mediation program, borrowers can stay in their homes and the mortgage continues to perform for the creditor. Florida's Mortgage Modification Mediation program ("MMM") began in the Middle District of Florida in 2010, and by 2013 the program had reached the Southern and Northern Districts.

Mortgage modifications can be accomplished on properties that are homestead properties under applicable state law, rental properties, property occupied by dependents of the borrower, inherited property, or property obtained through dissolution, even if the party seeking the modification is not a signatory on the note. MMM programs are generally eligible to individual debtors in Chapters 7, 11, 12, and 13 bankruptcy cases, who have paid their filing fees in full. Both represented and *pro se* debtors are eligible to participate. However, there is anecdotal evidence that the success rate is significantly greater when the debtor is represented by an attorney.

Generally, the MMM program in Florida works as follows: (1) The debtor makes "adequate protection" payments of 31% of his or her gross income, less any homeowners' association fees, to the lender. (2) Next, the debtor files a motion for referral to mediation within 90 days of filing the case. (3) After the motion is filed, the Court enters an *ex parte* order referring the parties to mediation and requiring the debtor to provide the lender with a package of information to be uploaded onto the MMM portal. Once the required information has been uploaded to the portal, the parties schedule a telephonic mediation.

Other MMM programs throughout the United States follow a similar track and maintain similar requirements. For instance, the programs in New York, New Jersey, Rhode Island, Pennsylvania, and Wisconsin all require payments in some amount that may be related to the amount of the debtor's income, set forth the time in which the request for mortgage modification should begin, and use a MMM portal to facilitate the exchange of documents and other information. During an interim trial payment period, the homeowner pays to the lender a monthly amount, calculated by the lender, which represents what the lender believes the modification payment will be.

The portal is a particularly important component to the MMM process. Prior to the establishment of the MMM portal, there were issues with communication and risk of lost documents. MMM packages were sent, lenders complained that the packages were not complete, and borrowers complained that they were sending the same documents multiple times. Moreover, without the portal, the borrowers had very little opportunity to communicate with the lender. This resulted in borrowers' paying trial payments for more than twelve months. Now, with the MMM portal, there is no question as to which documents are required and which documents have been uploaded. In addition, the borrower or the borrower's attorney can now communicate directly with the lender, and all of the communications are logged electronically and available for the mediator to review if needed.

In Florida, the order directing the parties to MMM gives them fourteen days to jointly select a qualified mediator. If the parties cannot agree on a mediator, the debtor may select a mediator, and the lender may object within seven days. If an objection to the mediator is timely filed, the Chapter 13 trustee (or in a Chapter 7 case, the Court clerk) will appoint a mediator from the Court's list of approved mediators. If the debtor is *pro se*, the Court may appoint a mediator.

The mediator's obligations are similar to obligations that exist in other proceedings. By way of example, the obligations in Florida are outlined in the order referring the matter to MMM. These include that the mediator shall (1) be governed by the standards of professional conduct set forth in the Florida rules for certified and court-appointed mediators and shall have judicial immunity to the same extent as a judge; (2) receive mediator's fees of $500.00 for preparation and participation in the first two hours of mediation, to be split equally between the debtor and the lender; (3) receive hourly compensation at an agreed hourly rate for any MMM conferences that extend beyond two one-hour conferences; (4) use the MMM portal to facilitate the exchange of information between the parties; (5) report on all mediation sessions on the portal; and (6) file a final report with the court within seven days after the final mediation, indicating whether an agreement was reached.

As with non-MMM mediations, there is a strong presumption of confidentiality in the MMM mediation process. Accordingly, all oral and written statements made by the parties, attorneys, and other participants at the mediation are privileged and confidential. All confidential statements cannot be reported, recorded, placed into evidence, made known to the Court, or construed as an admission.

The MMM mediation program also has a good-faith component. If parties do not engage in the MMM process in good faith, they could face possible damages or sanctions.[4]

---

4. In Florida, courts have not developed any clear standards for evaluating good faith in court-ordered mediations. *See* Procaps S.A. v. Patheon Inc., 2015 WL 3539737, at *7 (S.D. Fla. June 4, 2015).

Conclusion

While bankruptcy mediation is akin to other types of mediation, it is also unique in many ways. In consumer bankruptcy, debtors with little to lose could still lose everything they have. At the opposite end of the spectrum, in large Chapter 11, cases issues are complex and broad-ranging, potentially involving pensions, collective bargaining agreements, payments to creditors and the loss of equity, among other issues. What the mediation process brings to these issues is not just the avoidance of costly litigation, but a central arena to bring a host of complex issues and possibly multiple parties to the forefront in the most effective way possible. Parties get to be heard, but at the same time, a forum based upon bankruptcy knowledge and experience is established in which to create a roadmap for potential settlement.

A skilled, effective bankruptcy mediator can help counteract the financial damage to all parties that may otherwise result from delay in a situation involving economic distress. And while many of the principles of nonbankruptcy mediation apply, bankruptcy involves some unique aspects, to the potential benefit of all parties involved.

CHAPTER 7

Managing Post-Acquisition Disputes

John Levitske and Stephen H. Knee[1]

EDITOR'S NOTE: Too little attention has been paid to a delicate and consequential area of the M&A lawyer's practice: Drafting processes to manage disputes that may be anticipated to arise after the closing of an acquisition. These disputes may involve disagreements on valuation, questions of the accuracy of representations, or any number of contingencies that the parties agreed to as part of the deal, yet too often didn't think through in terms of the process to be followed in the event they come to different conclusions. This chapter takes a disciplined look at the topic from the perspective of two informed M&A practitioners—a lawyer and an expert witness, both of whom have also served as arbitrators.

In a merger or acquisition ("M&A"), the parties enter into a definitive acquisition agreement which details the agreed-upon terms of the transaction. These include the respective seller conveying the agreed-upon entity or assets to the buyer, and the respective buyer tendering the agreed-upon price, as well as certain limitations on liability between the parties. In addition, the agreement often includes dispute resolution process terms regarding (among others) pre-closing disputes, post-closing disputes, purchase price adjustment disputes, earn-out disputes and claims for indemnifications.

---

1. Statements and opinions expressed herein are solely those of the authors and may not coincide with those of Huron Consulting Group or Greenbaum Rowe. In addition, the authors acknowledge the contributions made to this publication by the following individuals who provided comments: Randy A. Bridgeman, Esq., Partner, Perkins Coie LLP, Chicago and David T. Cellitti, Esq., Partner, Quarles & Brady, LLP, Chicago; and who provided editorial assistance: John A. Taylor, ASA, CMC, Managing Director, Houlihan Lokey, Los Angeles and Amy Xia, Financial Analyst, Houlihan Lokey, Chicago.

This chapter provides a brief, summary introduction to managing the M&A dispute resolution process for private company post-closing disputes. This chapter discusses seven sub-topics:

- *How might transactional attorneys help clients avoid overlooking certain of the risks of post-closing disputes?*
- *What kinds of conflicts might arise before closing?*
- *What kinds of conflicts commonly arise after closing?*
- *Is it reasonable to expect transactional lawyers to familiarize themselves with suitable dispute resolution mechanisms and to negotiate suitable mechanisms into the acquisition agreement in the first instance?*
- *If so, what information do transactional lawyers need to know?*
- *Can best practices be articulated for practitioners in this area?*
- *As a threshold matter, is the problem of M&A-related disputes management perceived broadly enough, or is there a need to sensitize and train M&A lawyers to this risk?*

In contrast to the situation with private companies, alternative dispute resolution clauses are rare in public company acquisition agreements. This arises primarily from the fact that there are so many shareholders in a public company that it would be impractical to pursue claims against all the shareholders. That is why the structure of a public company acquisition uses breaches of representations and warranties and covenants as grounds for termination of the deal by the non-breaching party without recourse under an indemnification provision. With public companies, recourse against the breaching party may take the form of a claim for damages, as well as expense reimbursement and/or a breakup fee.

This chapter, however, focuses on alternative dispute resolution provisions in private company transactions.

How might transactional attorneys help clients avoid overlooking certain of the risks of post-closing disputes?

The dispute provisions in the agreement are matters of contract. Accordingly, transactional attorneys may help clients avoid certain of the risks of M&A disputes in these areas through carefully drafted provisions.

Generally, one of the objectives of the seller in a private company merger or acquisition is to limit its liability to the buyer, since the seller is giving up limited liability when operating in the corporate or limited liability company form. One of the objectives of the buyer is to obtain as much protection as it can through seller representations and warranties, and indemnification for their breaches as well as breaches of any covenants by the seller, thereby obtaining what the buyer bargained for in entering into the transaction in the first place. In addition, whether the agreed-to entity or assets are conveyed in full and the final quantification of the agreed-upon price are often subjects of dispute.

The seller often tries to limit the amount of liability for breaches of representations and warranties or post-closing covenants through deductibles and caps on liability and limitations on the survival of representations and warranties after closing, with recourse limited to the indemnification provision, except in cases of fraud or intentional misrepresentation. By contrast, the buyer tries to limit or eliminate any deductible or cap on damages, to allocate liability to the seller for matters relating to the pre-closing period, and to provide that the indemnification provision is not the exclusive remedy for alleged breaches by the seller. The role of the transactional counselor in each of these cases is self-evident. The resulting agreement should reflect intentional risk allocation, including the risk of delay and expense in the process by which anticipated disputes will be resolved.

What kinds of conflicts might arise before closing?

M&A disputes may occur pre-closing or post-closing. The acquisition agreement will give the buyer the right to terminate the agreement if the seller does not perform certain covenants or if there is a breach of representations or warranties pre-closing. Ordinarily the buyer will seek damages arising from the alleged breach. The agreement can provide for alternative dispute resolution in such pre-closing circumstances.

What kinds of conflicts commonly arise after closing?

This chapter focuses on post-closing disputes. After closing, issues may arise regarding quantification, compliance or accuracy, such as:

- Purchase price adjustment disputes
  - Closing working capital or closing net worth calculation disputes
  - Contingent additional purchase price/earn-out calculation disputes
- Breaches of seller's representation and warranty disputes
  - Capitalization
  - Customer or supplier contracts
  - Employees or benefits
  - Historical financial statements
  - Intellectual property
  - Undisclosed liabilities
  - Taxes
  - Environmental liabilities
- Specialty indemnification provision disputes
  - Environmental liabilities
  - Regulatory compliance issues
  - Taxes
- Covenant breach assertions
- Fraud assertions

Purchase price disputes normally arise pursuant to an explicit purchase price adjustment provision in the agreement. Closing working capital, closing net worth calculation disputes and contingent additional purchase price/earn-out calculation disputes often involve accounting or valuation quantification issues. Therefore, this process is normally handled by explicit alternative dispute resolution provisions in the agreement. There are many different types of dispute resolution mechanics. Most involve an independent third-party (typically an accountant or appraiser) who is appointed to determine the correct final calculation. The provision can name a specific accountant or appraiser, describe the type of firm (such as an accountant or appraiser with a nationally recognized consulting firm), or designate a specific firm. In the alternative, the agreement may permit each party to select an accountant or appraiser if they cannot agree on a single accountant or appraiser, and allow those two accountants or appraisers to choose a third accountant or appraiser with a majority (of the three) decision to prevail. There are other variations regarding the decision-maker in such provisions.

Jurisdiction is also an important consideration. The parties may wish to designate the accountant/appraiser as an arbitrator, and the process as an arbitration, to take advantage of federal and state arbitration statutes that provide for court enforcement of their decision. Disputes before the accountant or appraiser may be considered arbitrations under the Federal Arbitration Act ("FAA"), but are not always recognized as such by state courts. If a party seeks court intervention to enforce an arbitration agreement or enforce or vacate an arbitration award, state courts frequently have jurisdiction. Nevertheless, the FAA does not provide for federal personal or subject matter jurisdiction, which must be satisfied independently. In addition, the seller often seeks to have a clear distinction drawn in the agreement between claims and items covered by the purchase price adjustment dispute resolution process (and is within the agreed scope of the appointed accountant or appraiser) and other dispute resolution processes, to avoid the risks of double-counting.

Three other common categories of disputes—breaches of seller's representations and warranties, enforcement of specific indemnities, and covenant and fraud breaches—usually do not have an explicit alternative dispute resolution mechanism in the acquisition agreement. However, typically at a minimum, a process is specified for submitting indemnity claims under the agreement.

Is it reasonable to expect transactional lawyers to familiarize themselves with suitable alternative dispute resolution mechanisms and to negotiate suitable mechanisms into the acquisition agreement in the first instance?

Transactional attorneys may help clients manage certain of the risks of post-closing disputes by familiarizing themselves with available dispute resolution mechanisms, in addition to normal litigation, and attempting to negotiate to align the mechanisms in the acquisition agreement with the client's needs and perceived risks of the deal. Alternative dispute resolution provisions may or may not fit the specific situation and client's needs. Nevertheless, the use of alternative dispute resolution provisions is a deal-by-deal consideration that often requires a transactional lawyer to evaluate whether such provisions may be appropriate for a particular agreement.

If so, what information do transactional lawyers need to know?

Obviously, it will be helpful for the transactional lawyer to be informed by the client as to the client's needs and perceived risks of the deal. The dispute resolution process mechanism would be designed to serve those ends, from the available (not mutually exclusive) alternatives of:

- Negotiation,
- Mediation,
- Arbitration,
- Litigation,
- A phased approach of negotiation, mediation, and arbitration,
- Collaborative processes,
- A variation on some of the above, such as expert evaluation, early neutral evaluation, or advisory arbitration,
- A combination of some of the above.

Also, the selection of mechanism may vary, depending on whether an issue occurs pre-closing or post-closing.

Can best practices be articulated for practitioners in this area?

Generally, each transaction, client, and context has different needs and, therefore, different solutions. Nevertheless, some external resources are available that can assist transactional lawyers in the evaluation of whether or not an alternative dispute resolution provision makes sense in a particular situation and, if so, which type. The ABA Business Law Section, Mergers and Acquisitions (M&A) Committee provides publications and educational courses that may be helpful to the transactional lawyer seeking to develop his or her own best practices. For example, the M&A Committee publishes studies of common dispute issues arising in reported transactions. In addition, the M&A Committee publishes model acquisition agreements, including a model Stock Purchase Agreement and a model Asset Purchase Agreement, both of which are supplemented by the Committee's Commentary. The model Stock Purchase Agreement was updated in 2010 and the model Asset Purchase Agreement is currently in the process of being updated. Both models have detailed commentary relevant to these issues and considerations.[2]

In addition, the ABA Business Law Section Dispute Resolution (DR) Committee provides educational programs that cover considerations related to M&A disputes. Its recent programs have included topics such as Cross-Border Deals: State of the Art of International Negotiation, Mediation and Arbitration; Designing the Process for Resolution of Post-Merger & Acquisition Disputes: Smarter Consideration of People, Parties, Diversity, and Globalization in Selecting and Designing the Process; Whether Collaborative Law Can Be Used to Effectively and Efficiently Resolve Post-Merger and Acquisition Disputes; and Avoiding a Train Wreck: Best Practices for Multi-Tracked Litigation, Mediation, & Arbitration.[3]

As a threshold matter, is the M&A-related disputes management perceived broadly enough, or is there a need to sensitize and train M&A lawyers to this risk?

The issue appears to be perceived broadly enough among the M&A bar. However, important strategic opportunities exist for M&A counsel to enhance their practice. In this regard, M&A lawyers should take the opportunity to familiarize themselves with the current common issues and to be sensitive to the types of issues that may be relevant for the particular transactions they will encounter. In addition, clients themselves need to be cognizant of the risks of poorly drafted or erroneous dispute resolution provisions that may not work in practice, which are sometimes last-minute insertions of legacy language previously used because the client has chosen to not expend legal resources to do otherwise.

According to the current ABA M&A Committee, Deals Point Study Task Force, in a 2015 survey of 118 acquisitions of private companies by public companies in 2014, only 18 (or 15%) specified alternative dispute resolution for issues not covered by the explicit purchase price adjustment mechanism. Of those 18, four (or 22% of the subset) specified mediation, one (or 6% of the subset) specified mediation followed by

---

2. For information on the M&A Committee's publications, *see*: http://apps.americanbar.org/dch/committee.cfm?com=CL560000.

3. For information on the Dispute Resolution Committee's programs, *see*: http://www.americanbar.org/groups/dispute_resolution.html.

arbitration, and 13 (or 72% of the subset) specified arbitration; 14 (or 78% of the subset) specified a binding determination. Of the subset of 14 specified binding determinations, a specific arbiter was designated as the service provider in each of those deals. In the remaining 104 transactions, either the parties intentionally chose not to have alternative dispute resolution procedures for non-purchase price adjustment items specified in the agreement or failed to explore the opportunity to include such a provision. Those that did frequently provided for arbitration.[4]

Furthermore, according to the Shareholder Representative Services 2014 study of acquisitions of 700 private companies by private or public companies, about 27% of the disputed issues were covered by an explicit purchase price adjustment mechanism. In contrast, 57% of the dispute issues were related to breaches of representations and warranties claims not covered by alternative dispute resolution provisions.[5]

The current Committee Commentary supplementing the ABA Model Asset Acquisition Agreement lists the pros and cons of using alternative dispute resolution provisions, in the Commentary to Section 13.4 at page 256, as follows:

> *Factors that support exclusion of a mandatory binding arbitration clause include the following:*
> *(a) litigation is the appropriate dispute resolution mechanism because the buyer is more likely than the seller to assert claims under the acquisition agreement;*
> *(b) the prospect of litigation may give the buyer greater leverage with respect to resolving such claims than would the prospect of mandatory arbitration;*
> *(c) arbitration may promote an unfavorable settlement;*
> *(d) arbitration brings an increased risk of compromised compensatory damage awards;*
> *(e) arbitration lowers the likelihood of receiving high punitive damages;*
> *(f) certain provisional remedies (such as injunctive relief) may not be available in arbitration;*
> *(g) the arbitration decision may not be subject to meaningful judicial review;*

---

4. Preliminary survey information provided by ABA Business Law Section, M&A Committee, Deal Points Task Force, August 18, 2015. The 2014 Deal Points Study is still in process and was scheduled to be published later in 2015.

5. 2014 SRS Acquiom M&A Deal Terms Study, SRS Acquiom LLP, https://www.srsacquiom.com/resources/ma-deal-terms-study/ (last accessed February 25, 2016).

(h) rules of discovery and evidence (unavailable in some arbitration proceedings) may favor the buyer's position; [and]

(i) because many of the facts necessary for favorable resolution of the buyer's claims may be in the seller's possession (especially if a dispute centers on representations and warranties containing knowledge qualifications), these facts may not be available to the buyer without full discovery.

Factors that would encourage inclusion of a mandatory binding arbitration clause in a buyer's initial draft include the following:

(a) arbitration may promote a reasonable settlement;

(b) arbitration may reduce costs;

(c) arbitration creates the possibility of keeping the dispute confidential;

(d) arbitrators may be more sophisticated in business affairs than judges or juries and reach a more appropriate result;

(e) arbitration may be speedier than litigation;

(f) arbitration eliminates any home-court advantage to a seller litigating in its own jurisdiction;

(g) arbitration is a less confrontational environment and may better maintain the business relations of the buyer and the seller;

(h) arbitration furnishes an opportunity to have special experts selected by the parties rule on technical issues; and

(i) arbitration decreases the risk of punitive damages.

Consequently, important strategic opportunities exist for M&A counsel to enhance the situation, such as:

- Initiating negotiation of a clear and advantageous dispute resolution plan of specific and suitable scope, including alternative dispute resolution processes if appropriate, as part of the agreement.
- When a dispute arises, even if there is no alternative dispute resolution provision in the agreement:
  - Providing advice before opportunities to influence the outcome are diminished,
  - Advising the client regarding the costs,[6] control, and timing consequences of alternatives to seeking court intervention,

---

6. One of the cost considerations may also include whether insurance coverage exists for transaction-related claims.

- Strategizing to avoid waiver of procedural deficiencies, if any, such as extension of time issues, and
- Providing input on the selection of and into the engagement letter for an arbitrator, mediator, joint expert, or collaborative neutral, as appropriate.

CHAPTER **8**

Family Business Disputes and Business Divorces

Stephen H. Knee[1]

EDITOR'S NOTE: As Stephen Knee points out, most American businesses are small and privately owned. Disputes arising among partners, shareholders, and closely held entities are often particularly emotional and, if not skillfully handled, can be destructive not only to the business but to some of the most important relationships in the lives of the disputants. New Jersey attorney Knee helps lawyers plan, counsel, and protect clients' interests in these delicate matters and also mediates business divorces and other business disputes.

Introduction

Most businesses in the United States are privately owned. Some are family-owned, some are not. These businesses operate in various forms—some as corporations, some as partnerships, some as limited partnerships, some as limited liability partnerships, some as limited liability limited partnerships, some as limited liability companies, and some as sole proprietorships.

Being in business with another party is a marriage. As in any marriage, different people approach things in different ways, have

---

1. This chapter is drawn heavily from the Introduction and Chapters 1, 2, and 10 of STEPHEN H. KNEE, BUSINESS DIVORCE: UNDERSTANDING ITS DYNAMICS AND FORMULATING SOLUTIONS (A.B.A. 2015) and appears with the permission of the American Bar Association.

different views on the same subject, and handle relationships differently. If the business is a family business, family dynamics come into play and complicate the relationships. It is therefore important to provide for governance, succession planning, and exit strategies for participants at the time the business is formed and memorialize this in a written agreement to be updated as circumstances change. It is in many ways the same as a prenuptial agreement entered into before marriage. Unfortunately, it is quite common when these businesses are formed for the founders to neither make the time, nor to have the desire to spend the funds necessary to take this step until after business formation. In those situations, a breakup can become a costly and prolonged process.

Typical Fact Patterns

Two individuals form a business. One has expertise in the normal back-office functions, the other is a great salesperson. Over the years, one of the individuals begins to feel that she is contributing much more to the business than the other individual and that it is unfair, since both are drawing the same salaries and are fifty-fifty owners. This resentment results in the individuals barely communicating with each other, adversely affecting the performance of the business. The decision-making process becomes deadlocked—the resentment builds until there is an event that pushes the first individual over the cliff. The battle has begun.

Two individuals form a business. Over the years, some, but not all, of their children join the business. After the founders pass away, the business continues to be run by some of those children. All of the children inherit their proportionate share of each parent's 50% interest. The children running the business pay themselves generous salaries, leaving almost no income to be distributed to the other equity owners. This is resented by those equity owners. The resentment builds up until one or more can no longer tolerate the situation, and an expensive and time-consuming lawsuit claiming shareholder oppression results.

Two individuals form a business. One has expertise in international transactions, the other is a great salesperson and runs the domestic operations. Over the years, one of the individuals begins to feel that she is contributing much more to the business than the other individual and that it is unfair to her. She feels that she's entitled to a higher salary and gradually begins to increase it, have the business pay many of her expenses and employ members of her family. The second individual is passive by nature and turns a blind eye to the situation. When the business was formed, the individuals entered into a shareholders' agreement containing buy-sell provisions. The agreement provided a formula to arrive at the purchase price in the event the buyout mechanism was triggered. The agreement provided for a voluntary buyout during life and a mandatory buyout on the individual's death to be partially funded by life insurance. The passive individual was older than the other and eventually developed a life-threatening disease. The healthy individual made an offer to purchase the interest of the passive individual at a purchase price that was unacceptable. As happens in a great number of closely held businesses, the buy-sell agreement was never updated and the formula remained unchanged. The healthy individual objected to paying under the formula, since he felt that it would result in a purchase price much higher than he thought was fair. Since the parties could not reach agreement, the healthy individual brought suit to reform the formula in the buy-sell agreement. The court held that there was no legal basis to reform the agreement. The healthy individual then commenced an arbitration proceeding pursuant to the arbitration clause in the buy-sell agreement. The arbitrator also held there was no legal basis to reform the agreement and the parties were stuck with their bargain. When the passive individual passed away many years later, the healthy individual advised the widow that he would not under any circumstances pay the purchase price computed under the formula. As leverage, he also refused to turn over the life insurance proceeds on the passive individual's life to his widow. This time, the widow brought an arbitration proceeding that, after much expense and the passage of a great deal of time, resulted in the healthy individual being required to turn over the insurance proceeds and to pay the purchase price computed in accordance with the formula.

An individual formed a business that became very successful. He had two children, a daughter and a son. After college, the son went into the business; the daughter did not. When the daughter married, her husband became an employee. The father's will left the business to his children in equal shares. After their father's death, the brother became chief executive of the company. The brother had always felt that his brother-in-law was extremely lazy and never performed his job, but did nothing while his father was still alive. After his father's death, the brother began increasing his own salary and, after what he regarded as a suitable time, fired the brother-in-law. The brother did not allow the company to pay any dividends and, since the daughter was not an employee, she did not receive any return on her equity interest in the business. The sister brought suit, claiming that it was her reasonable expectation that her husband would continue to be employed, that she would become a member of the Board of Directors, and that dividends would be paid to her. The sister prevailed in this costly litigation, with the court holding that the brother's conduct amounted to shareholder oppression and ordering the reinstatement of the husband, the resumption of dividends, and the appointment of the daughter to the Board.

A husband and wife formed a business. They had two children, a daughter and a son. Both children worked in the business, as did the daughter's husband. When the father retired, he and his wife sold their shares equally to both children. The brother-in-law started another venture while he was still employed by the business and had that business provide startup capital, as well as loans, to his new venture. The new venture began to take up more and more of the brother-in-law's time. The brother put up with this for some time, but finally lost his temper and fired the brother-in-law. Costly litigation followed. The court appointed a fiscal agent, to be paid for by the business, to oversee the business until the matter was resolved. The matter was finally settled through mediation, with the sister buying out her brother.

An individual formed a business and employed his son. The business prospered and the father and son got along beautifully. The son met a young woman and eventually became engaged. His mother disliked his fiancée and kept haranguing the father to have the son break the engagement. When this didn't work, she turned the father against the son, and the father fired the son. The son immediately started the exact same business, solicited the father's business' customers and sold the exact same product. The father's business suffered greatly, and he brought suit to enjoin this alleged unfair competition. The father prevailed, but the family was destroyed.

A father, son, father-in-law and son-in-law were in business together. The business began to have financial difficulties. The father was CEO and fired the son-in-law. The son-in-law started the exact the same business. The father-in-law started diverting inventory and orders to the son-in-law's new business. The father's business suffered financially, defaulted on its loan with its bank and the bank commenced suit. The court appointed a fiscal agent to liquidate the company's assets. The fiscal agent employed counsel and accountants to assist in the liquidation. All of the assets were consumed in paying the costs of the liquidation, the fees of the fiscal agent, counsel, accountants, and the bank loan—the father and son received nothing.

Four brothers started a real estate business. There was no written agreement between them regarding the business. The eldest brother owned the largest equity interest (40%), by virtue of his being the eldest, and the three younger brothers had lesser equal shares (20% each). Although these brothers could outvote the eldest if they voted as a block, they never did, since the family culture was that the eldest always ran the show. The business ran smoothly while all the brothers were alive. Real estate taxes were payable quarterly and each family sent its share, based on each family's percentage ownership, to the eldest, who paid the taxes. Income from the business was distributed by the eldest brother according to the percentage ownership. When one of the brothers died, his family refused to pay its share of the real estate taxes. The rest paid their share plus the share of the defaulting family, and sued that family for the unpaid sum. The defaulting family counterclaimed for dissolution of the business. The trial court refused to dissolve the business. The appellate court reversed and ordered the sale of the properties and distribution of the proceeds and remanded the case to the trial court. The trial court appointed a retired judge as trustee to conduct the liquidation. The trustee retained one of his colleagues as his counsel and also retained an accountant. Each family also hired counsel. The liquidation process took many years. New trustees came and went. Disputes developed between the families and between members of individual families that required separate counsel, resulting in a real horror story with millions of dollars spent on professional fees and, most likely, a number of lost opportunities.

An Ounce of Prevention Is Worth a Pound of Cure

Whatever the form of the business, every closely held business should have an agreement between the parties regarding governance, buying and selling interests in the business, and dispute resolution. This will be helpful in avoiding disputes between the parties in the running of the business by having clear lines of authority and providing a mechanism to aid in the resolution of other problems that arise when circumstances change and one or more owners become disgruntled.

The document that accomplishes this in the corporate setting is called the shareholders' agreement and covers matters of governance as well as buying and selling interests in the business and the method of dispute resolution. If the entity is a limited liability company or partnership (whether general, limited, limited liability, or limited liability limited), the governance provisions, as well as the buy-sell and dispute resolution provisions, would be specified in the limited liability company agreement, operating agreement, or partnership agreement.

Governance

Corporations

A corporation is managed by or under the direction of its Board of Directors. The Board of Directors sets the policy to be carried out by the officers elected by the Board and must approve matters not in the ordinary course of business.

In a closely held corporation, the shareholders will often agree to vote for the nominees selected by the owners as members of the board. The shareholders' agreement can provide that the number of directors to be nominated by each shareholder be proportional to the ownership interest of each owner, thereby reflecting his or her percentage ownership interest in the composition of the board. Modern corporation statutes usually permit directors to have different numbers of votes, thereby eliminating the need for the election of non-owner directors to accomplish the proportional representation in corporate decisions. The certificate of incorporation can provide for greater shareholder voting requirements than the number provided as a default in the corporation statute of the state of incorporation (usually a majority) for items such as mergers and acquisitions, sales of assets other than in the ordinary course of business, and amendments of the certificate of incorporation, as well as requiring a similar shareholder vote for bylaw amendments, loans, and matters not usually requiring shareholder approval but are important to minority shareholders. While this may protect minority shareholders by giving them veto power over these items, it can lead to deadlock between the majority and minority owners and result in a business divorce. Therefore, care should be taken in using such provisions.

Limited Liability Companies and Partnerships

Limited liability companies can be either member managed or manager managed. If member managed, the voting would normally be proportionate to each member's ownership interest. If manager managed, the manager or managers would be given the authority and the number of votes set forth in the limited liability company or operating agreement that can be proportioned to each member's ownership interest. In the partnership context, the provisions would be set forth in the partnership or limited partnership agreement, as the case may be.

The limited liability or operating agreement or partnership or limited partnership agreement can also provide for greater member voting requirements than provided as a default (usually a majority interest in profits or in some states a simple majority) in the formation statute of the state of formation for items such as mergers and acquisitions, sales of assets other than in the ordinary course of business, and amendments of the limited liability or operating agreement or partnership or limited partnership agreement, as well as loans and other matters. This can lead to the same problems described above in the corporate setting.

Dispute Resolution Provisions

The shareholders' agreement, limited liability agreement or operating agreement or partnership agreement should also provide a mechanism for dispute resolution among the equity owners, namely mediation and arbitration (or mediation and then arbitration if the mediation is not successful), once the dispute becomes unresolvable despite good-faith direct negotiation. The agreement can also provide for a provisional director in the corporate setting and its equivalent in the limited liability company and partnership settings to settle governance questions before they become unresolvable. The provisional director or its equivalent can cast the deciding vote when governance questions cannot be resolved because the decision makers are equally divided.

Buy-Sell Provisions

The buy-sell provisions should deal with buying and selling business interests during lifetime as well as upon death.

In the closely held business setting, equity owners normally choose whom they want to be in business with, and accordingly, these owners do not want any interest sold to a third party without their consent. However, equity owners also do not want to be stuck with non-liquid assets that may constitute the majority of their wealth until the other owners consent to a sale. Therefore, most buy-sell provisions provide for a limited right to sell during lifetime. Giving the other owners (1) a means of protecting their desire to keep ownership within the group unless they consent to the sale and or (2) the right to buyout an owner desiring to sell if they do not want him to sell to a third party, allows owners wanting to sell the needed flexibility and also provides a mechanism to avoid costly litigation if a dispute between equity owners has become unresolvable.

During lifetime, the items to be considered in a buy-sell provision are as follows:

(a) Permitting a sale of an owner's interest with all of the other owners' consent;

(b) Triggering Events for a buy-out;

(c) Price, or method of determining price; and

(d) Payment Terms and Security.

All agreements should provide for a mandatory buyout of a deceased equity owner upon her death. The reasons for this are twofold: (1) being a closely held business, there is no established market for its equity interests, resulting in illiquidity to the heirs of the deceased owner leading to their becoming unhappy minority owners with no way out, and (2) the remaining owners may not want to be in business with the deceased owner's heirs whom they did not select as partners in the first place. In the alternative, an optional buyout may be provided in the agreement.

The agreement will deal with the following with respect to buyouts triggered by the death of an equity owner:

(a) Price or method of determining price;

(b) Funding; and

(c) Payment Terms and Security.

The sales price can be based on book value, formula driven or agreed to by the owners and set forth in an addendum to be periodically updated, with a formula as a backup if the addendum is not periodically updated. If book value is used, it will result in an insufficient price in a business having little or no hard assets or in a hard asset-rich business where the hard assets have been depreciated below market value and have not been adjusted to market value in computing the purchase price. In that case, a formula-driven valuation is preferable. The formula most commonly used is a multiple of earnings for that type of business. The formula could also be based on a multiple of sales, if appropriate for that industry. Another method is to have each party pick an appraiser, with both appraisers picking a third appraiser, and having the majority determine the valuation (or having the third appraiser make the determination).

The buy-sell provisions of the agreement should be reviewed annually to avoid future problems. For instance, changed circumstances may make the valuation method no longer fair for one or all of the parties. Failure to update the set price or the formula may create problems in the future, such as one or more of the parties' refusing to honor their obligations.

Although business considerations usually drive the agreement, appreciating the tax consequences in advance can avoid unnecessary disputes. Therefore, tax counsel, or a tax accountant experienced in these matters, should be consulted in the drafting stage.

Methods of Resolution

The best solution to disputes in a business breakup would be a negotiated agreement. However, since negotiations often take place after a problem has developed, issues that could have been directly resolved have disappeared and the issues remaining have become intractable.

ADR

Alternate Dispute Resolution ("ADR") may be the best answer. ADR is private and confidential. This is especially important where the parties do not want the proceedings made public. Court proceedings create a public record. The reasons for wanting confidentiality can be manyfold; not wanting customers to know that the equity owners are fighting, which could hurt business; keeping proprietary information from getting into the hands of competitors; keeping financial information private; or maintaining the business participants and strategies private, among others. In court litigation, the dispute will become public knowledge and, in most cases, anything filed in the proceeding, with some exceptions, may be subject to access by any member of the public, including competitors— often, depending on the jurisdiction, an online click away.

Also, when using private alternatives to the courts, the parties may choose a mediator or arbitrator, as the case may be, familiar with business disputes of this type and, in appropriate cases, the industry involved, rather than being assigned to a judge who may not be familiar either with such business disputes or such industry.

The two most popular methods of ADR are mediation and arbitration.

Mediation is a procedure to settle a legal dispute with the help of a third-party neutral, trained to facilitate a resolution of the dispute that is acceptable to all the parties. The mediator helps define the issues and helps the parties resolve those issues on terms that they devise. Mediation can be facilitative, where the mediator's function is to move the parties toward agreement, or evaluative, where the mediator gives each party an evaluation of the strengths and weaknesses of their position to help them come to an agreement, or both. Any agreement reached is purely voluntary; unlike an arbitrator, a mediator has no power to require that a party accept an outcome that he or she finds unacceptable. The requirement to mediate can be set forth in the shareholders' agreement or the limited liability or operating agreement or partnership agreement or set forth in an agreement entered into after the dispute has matured.

Arbitration is a binding procedure that is adjudicative. In arbitration, a neutral or neutrals decide the dispute. The arbitrators can authorize discovery similar to, but presumably more limited and less expensive than, litigation and decide motions, hear witnesses, and, after a hearing, render a decision in writing. Unless the arbitration agreement requires it, the decision need not provide findings of fact or conclusions of law. The arbitration can be required by the agreement governing the transaction, or an agreement to arbitrate may be entered into after the dispute has matured. The arbitrator's decision is legally binding and can be converted to an enforceable court judgment. The arbitrator's decision is usually not appealable in court.

Arbitration was used long before mediation came into vogue as an alternative to litigation. However, a number of practitioners grew skeptical that the arbitrator or arbitrators would cut the baby down the middle in order, in their judgment, to be fair and accordingly shunned arbitration.

Over the years, the legal culture has changed, and many business lawyers have concluded that mediation is the preferable way to resolve a business dispute. This is especially true in the case of a business divorce.

Mediation is private. Outside parties do not have any knowledge of the existence of the dispute or that the parties are trying to resolve it. Proprietary and other confidential information is kept confidential. The parties can craft their own solution, as long as the solution is not illegal, whereas in arbitration and litigation, the parties may be bound by statutory and case law governing the situation. The transaction costs of mediation are a tiny fraction of the costs of adjudicative processes. Mediation opens up a whole world of creative solutions that are not available in either arbitration or litigation. The parties can pick their own mediator, either a business lawyer or accountant, rather than have a judge with unknown business experience. Also, since the parties are the ones crafting the solution, rather than an arbitrator or judge or jury, the parties are more likely to buy into the result. The mediation agreement should set a reasonable time limit to allow the parties to attempt to reach an agreement before the mediation must be terminated. Therefore, the parties should know early on whether or not an agreement can be reached. If not, the parties can terminate the mediation and move on to another forum set forth in the agreement (arbitration or litigation) for final and binding resolution. This saves time and expense, since an agreement will be reached expeditiously or else the proceeding will be terminated. If an agreement is reached, the parties can get back to business, thus reducing the cost of fighting (both financial and emotional), eliminating the risk (win or lose), minimizing the disruption of business and, often, preserving the relationship.

Binding arbitration shares some of the same benefits as mediation, such as privacy, confidentiality, and the ability to pick an arbitrator or arbitrators experienced in the subject of the dispute. The Federal Arbitration Act and state arbitration acts promote its use in the belief that arbitration provides a cheaper and faster resolution of a dispute than litigation. However, the grounds for appeal of arbitration awards are extremely limited. A mistake of law is generally not grounds for appeal, and in most instances appeals have been costly, time-consuming, and unsuccessful.

Many business lawyers have concluded that, as modern practice has become more complex, arbitration has begun to take on many of the attributes of litigation, and, as a practical matter, has not always lived up to its potential as a clear alternative to court. In many cases, modern arbitration has not been faster or cheaper than litigation. It is sometimes difficult to have consecutive days of hearings, due to the arbitrator's unavailability. This is especially true in situations where there is a panel of three arbitrators, since their schedules may conflict. Lawyers, just as in court, do most of the presentations. Thus, the goal of expeditious disposition of the dispute on commercially rational terms, is in many, cases not accomplished. Also, the cost of arbitration is often not less than the cost of litigation due to the fact that the arbitrator or arbitrators have not limited discovery, permitting much the same type of document exchange and depositions as in litigation and permitting much the same motion practice as in litigation. Over the last number of years, this problem has become exacerbated by the advent of electronic discovery. This also extended the time and increased the cost of the arbitration, thus eliminating two of its main advantages.

Recently, the major arbitration providers have been pushing what is referred to as "muscular arbitration." The concept is to encourage arbitrators to limit discovery, enforce more efficient means of presenting a case (i.e., offering direct examination of witnesses in advance in written form, subject to oral cross-examination), and tightening time schedules to finish the proceeding. Time will tell whether such procedural modifications will be successful.

Lawyers are trained that the best way to resolve an intractable dispute is through litigation. This is especially true if a party wants to delay resolution of the matter or to harass and bully the party with less resources through extensive motion practice and extensive discovery using what is commonly called the "scorched-earth tactic" or "Rambo litigation." Also, some practitioners feel that it is in their client's interest to commence litigation to have a receiver or fiscal agent appointed by the court to take control of the business or, in the latter case, to monitor the business and to increase the pressure on the defendant to settle on terms advantageous to the plaintiff.

The main advantage litigation has over arbitration is that a decision by a trial court can be appealed and may be overturned for mistakes of law or determinations against the weight of the evidence. Also, the judge and jury are paid with public funds, rather than by the parties. Besides the added cost and the amount of time involved in deciding disputes arising in closely held businesses through litigation, the real disadvantage of litigation over mediation is in a situation where there is "shareholder oppression" (where one party's tactics in the dispute is deemed by the court to be oppressive to the other party). The court, whether by statute or under the court's general equity power, can order the sale of one of one party's equity interest to the other party and set the price as well as the payment terms. This involuntary sale by one of the parties without the ability of the seller to agree on the price and the terms of sale may result in a lower price and less satisfactory payment terms than could be achieved in a private sale. In the extreme case, the court can order dissolution and liquidation, which is disadvantageous to all parties.

While litigation is not a bad choice in every case, it is in most, and the realities of being a closely held business, counsel for the inclusion of mediation, arbitration, or both in the governing documents.

CHAPTER 9

Dispute Resolution Considerations in Intellectual Property Cases

Kristine Dorrain, Sandra Partridge, and Ryan Isenberg

EDITOR'S NOTE: Until very recently, intellectual property disputes were considered the domain of the courts. Practitioners assumed that the nature of such assets, and the damages that could flow from breaches of agreements or unauthorized use, required the sort of equitable relief that could be obtained only from a judge. As these authors show, however, business practicalities have forced IP attorneys to reconsider how to serve their clients in a different way.

Introduction

The resolution of disputes over intellectual property ("IP") issues presents unique challenges. While intellectual property is generally thought of as encompassing patents, trademarks, copyrights, and trade secrets, the actual practice of intellectual property law implicates general business contracting in the form of license agreements for patented technology, distribution of trademarked merchandise, and sales of copyrighted software, in addition to the traditional topics of validity and infringement. Franchise agreements deal with trademarks, trade dress (the look and feel of a store or product), and even trade secrets (secret recipes, for instance). Employment agreements often protect trade secrets such as business methods or customer lists or assignments of IP ownership to the employer.

Because the practice of intellectual property law is so richly varied, the options for the resolution of disputes implicating that field present unique challenges for the lawyer advising a client. Despite the fact that most types of intellectual property disputes can be resolved through alternative dispute resolution, practical considerations may weigh against alternative dispute resolution ("ADR") even if there are significant benefits.[1] For instance, while there may be significant advantages to patent, trademark, and copyright infringement arbitration or mediation, most infringement claims are not against a party with whom the IP owner has a present contract or arbitration agreement, making a post-dispute agreement to arbitrate necessary. Additionally, invalidity defenses are best raised with the United States Patent and Trademark Office or the Register of Copyrights.

This chapter will present the benefits of different types of ADR in various forms of IP disputes. Each benefit will be followed by practical considerations when deciding whether to select ADR and what type of ADR to select. Ideally, the business lawyer will read this chapter prior to drafting an ADR clause; this chapter is addressed to the lawyer either deciding to include an ADR clause or deciding whether a post-dispute agreement to arbitration is desired.

Dispute Avoidance

Intellectual property attorneys negotiate agreements that are frequently lengthy and complex and focus on the terms of the working relationship between the parties, often skipping over dispute avoidance entirely.

Dispute avoidance can be encouraged in the contracting stage by reaching true agreement on terms. True agreement is reached by bringing both contracting parties into alignment on the contract's terms rather

---

1. In order to arbitrate or mediate a dispute, the parties must agree. This agreement can be made as part of another contract between the parties that contemplates future disputes. The clause is typically called a "pre-dispute agreement" because it is frequently drafted before the parties have a dispute, usually as part of the initial contract. If the dispute has already arisen, but the parties want to take advantage of the speed, efficiency, or expertise of ADR, they may agree after the dispute has arisen in a "post-dispute agreement to arbitrate (or mediate)." Either way, the parties have significant power over the process, including how fast any hearing will take place, who will decide the dispute, the choice of law, and the venue. The neutral only has the power granted to it by the parties' agreement.

than having a contract laced with accepted but not negotiated terms, such as through the eleventh-hour inclusion of boilerplate language.

Facilitated negotiation, using a mediator as part of the contract negotiations, can be a highly effective ADR technique in creating an understanding about the responsibilities and rewards of a contract that prevents subsequent disputes.

Fact-finding and early neutral evaluation are ADR techniques that can help avoid a dispute where additional accurate information is missing, and its absence has led to misunderstanding. Disputes about royalty payments, for example, can be avoided when a fact-finder or neutral evaluator discovers a contract where a term is vague or a process is unclear or outdated, and a remedy is devised among the parties before a misunderstanding becomes a costly and relationship-damaging dispute.

Patent Disputes

There are several different types of patent disputes. The most common are patent infringement by a third-party or a contracted (licensed) party, actions for invalidity by an alleged infringer or third-party, and license violations regarding sale or use of patented technology. Because patent disputes frequently involve specific technology or scientific issues best understood by a trained specialist, a key benefit of ADR is the selection of a qualified neutral rather than a generalist such as a judge. Where a thorough understanding of the technology or relevant art is important, the parties can select a neutral who has the requisite knowledge and experience that a judicial generalist might lack. The selection of a neutral with this specific background can save the parties significant time and money on expert witnesses who might be needed to bring a fact-finder up to speed at a *Markman* hearing,[2] for instance. Additionally, if claim construction or trade secrets are at issue, ADR presents a unique opportunity to use different expert neutrals when needed or preferred. One arbitrator can be chosen to hear the case, but it is entirely possible to have a separate arbitrator appointed to determine claim construction or the presence of a trade secret, subsequently providing

---

2. A *Markman* hearing occurs early in patent litigation where claim construction is at issue and the scope of patent claims needs to be adjudicated before the case can proceed on its merits regarding infringement or invalidity, for instance.

the findings to the case's arbitrator for the evidentiary hearing. Using a Web-based tool designed to help parties create an ADR clause can be very helpful by providing a convenient starting point for discussions regarding options.[3]

If there is a license in place and the parties desire to continue their relationship but need some issues resolved, mediation is an excellent solution. Mediation is non-binding and allows the parties to reach settlement on some or all of their disputes with a facilitator. A specially trained mediator can help the parties see their way to creative solutions that a generalist might miss. Mediation (culminating in a private agreement) and arbitration (culminating in an enforceable adjudication) are often used sequentially in a hybrid process known as med-arb, where arbitration follows a mediation impasse on some or all of the issues. If desired, the parties can use the same neutral in order to expedite the process; issues of neutrality and confidentiality have made this process less popular in the United States than in other jurisdictions, particularly in Asia and Europe.

A non-binding advisory arbitration supplies the parties with an award that, while unenforceable, may prompt a settlement or even a withdrawal of a claim. Additionally, mock arbitrations with only one side participating may be used to evaluate the likelihood of success at an actual hearing.

A common misconception of arbitration is that arbitrators "split the baby." However, in practice, that is rarely the case.[4] Typically, one party or the other will prevail. The award may not be the full amount requested by the prevailing party, but the same is true with verdicts rendered at the end of litigation in court. Additionally, parties to an arbitration can select either the arbitrator (in their ADR clause or by agreement during the arbitration) or have the opportunity to veto arbitrators selected by the other party.[5] Remedies available to parties in arbitration are the same as in court and may include injunctions, including temporary injunctions, awards of costs and fees, specific performance, and traditional monetary remedies. Arbitrations are

---

3. One of the authors is most familiar with the one provided by FORUM: www.adrforum.com/ClauseGenerator.

4. *See, e.g.,* https://www.adr.org/aaa/ShowPDF?doc=ADRSTG_014040. Claudia T. Solomon, *Splitting the Baby in International Arbitration,* NAT. L. J. (Jan. 19, 2015), https://www.lw.com/mediaCoverage/splitting-the-baby-in-international-arbitration, further highlights the growing role that dispositive motions are playing in modern arbitrations.

5. If an ADR provider is selected, there is typically a prescribed process for selecting the arbitrator or panel that allows each party to nominate or reject arbitrators from a list.

final—appeals are rare and based on narrow grounds, allowing parties to move past litigation without the concern of multiple trials.[6] Another benefit of arbitration and mediation is that settlements and awards are usually private. Where trade secrets are implicated (see trade secret section, below) or the result of an award would harm a party's reputation, the confidentiality of the process and outcome can be a significant incentive to utilize ADR.

A word about the United States Patent and Trademark Office's ("USPTO") America Invents Act ("AIA") Trials such as post-grant proceedings and *inter partes* review. The AIA trials are substantially similar to arbitration and resolve disputes over the validity of patent claims, conducted by experts under the auspices of the USPTO. It is proving to be a fast, efficient process.[7] Parties who utilized an AIA trial process, and were pleased with the results, will likely be equally satisfied with arbitrating any infringement dispute that might remain after the AIA trial is completed. Because the parties are unlikely to have a pre-existing relationship, agreeing to arbitrate the remaining issues would require a post-dispute agreement. A key benefit of arbitration is the speed and efficiency that the parties can utilize to quickly resolve their disputes and achieve an award. Parties run their own calendar and are not subject to the delays of the court. In many cases, parties can get to a full hearing in six months or less, if discovery is not an issue.

On the topic of hybrid or joint processes, counsel should remember that the parties grant the neutral the power they want the neutral to have. So creative ADR clause drafting can relegate certain disputes to courts and others to ADR. It is not an all-or-nothing process.

Practical Considerations

In many instances, the most pressing concern, regardless of the form of intellectual property being infringed or disclosed, is the need to get the claimed infringement to stop. Regardless of the form the intellectual property takes, quite often the fastest and most economical way to get the infringing activity to stop is to march into court, appear in front

---

6. But the inability to appeal an arbitration award in the absence of "manifest disregard" for the law can also be seen by some parties as a risk. *See* 9 U.S.C. § 10(a).

7. *See* http://www.uspto.gov/patents-application-process/patent-trial-and-appeal-board/trials. Most AIA trials are concluded in under twelve months, with many concluding in as few as six months.

of a judge, and ask for an immediate restraining order. Once that's in place, any form of ADR can be used to resolve the issue of damages or negotiate a license.

Though an arbitrator, or arbitration panel, may be empowered to issue an injunction, and indeed, most arbitration providers' Rules have a defined and expedited process for this, enforcing the injunction could prove troublesome. The big hammer the courts wield is the ability to hold a party in civil contempt for violating the injunction. Contempt violations may include fines, penalties, disgorgement, and most importantly, incarceration.[8] Indeed, the mere threat of incarceration can severely modify the behavior of even the most daring of litigants.[9] Finally, arbitrators only have power over those parties that agreed to be bound by the arbitration, whereas a dispute involving secondary infringers, even if the primary infringer is somehow bound by an arbitration provision, gets the party potentially only half a loaf.

Trademark (and Trade Dress) Disputes

As with patent disputes, trademark disputes can arise in the context of a contract, including a licensing or franchise agreement, or between parties who have no previous relationship. Counsel may think that a specially trained neutral is unnecessary to resolve trademark disputes, particularly when compared to the patent field. However, trademark law also has unique features that are remarkably suited to the specialized, privatized processes available in ADR. For example, franchise relationships are frequently fraught with tension and a shared interest to continue the relationship amicably and without public decisions. Mediation provides the parties with a safe space to resolve their disputes and can provide the ability for creative arrangements that allow the parties to continue their business relationship; additionally, mediation is often faster and cheaper than arbitration and can seem much less adversarial to the parties.

---

8. ClearOne Communs., Inc. v. Bowers, 643 F.3d 735 (10th Cir. Utah 2011) (incarceration ordered in trade secret case); ClearOne Communs., Inc. v. Bowers, 651 F.3d 1200, 1209 (10th Cir. Utah 2011) (affirming incarceration of non-party); Innovation Ventures, LLC v. N2G Distrib., Inc., 2013 U.S. Dist. LEXIS 68916 (E.D. Mich. May 15, 2013) (court will order disgorgement, daily fines, and incarceration, if Jeffrey Diehl fails to comply with this order.).

9. These are all still available, through the courts, for violating an arbitrator-ordered injunction, but it would require the additional step of litigation to enforce the order.

Trademark mediators and arbitrators are often practitioners who have themselves argued and defended likelihood of confusion and dilution claims. They understand the nuanced interplay between the U.S. federal common law of trademarks, state trademark law, and the Lanham Act. Pursuant to most rules promulgated by arbitration provider organizations, arbitrators can enjoin parties from infringing and can award monetary remedies for infringement.[10] Trademark neutrals have the ability to conduct site visits to view trade dress first-hand. While an arbitrator cannot invalidate a trademark, arbitration is often an excellent next step for the infringement portion of a dispute where the validity of the trademark has already been confirmed by the USPTO's Trademark Trial and Appeal Board or by a court.

Practical Considerations

A showing of irreparable harm entitles the trademark owner to an injunction against the infringing behavior, and it may be that a permanent injunction is all a brand owner is seeking. Many arbitration panelists are reluctant to issue a permanent injunction that could mean they are retaining semi-permanent jurisdiction over a matter long after a case concludes. In such a case, the courts may be the best solution.

Parties to all forms of intellectual property disputes may need a court's compulsory discovery process, especially as it relates to third parties. Federal courts in particular provide litigants with the easy ability to issue subpoenas nationwide. A complication that can arise from an arbitrator-issued subpoena is that involvement of a court may be required in order for the subpoena itself to be enforced. A party seeking discovery through a state court may first be obliged to get a subpoena issued from the court that is the proper venue for enforcement of the arbitration award, which potentially adds layers of cost and time, and provides avenues for opposition.

Additionally, certain trademark-specific problems may be better suited to intervention by courts where particular infringing activities are targeted. For example, professional sports franchises do not want unlicensed merchandise sold around the area where a championship is being held and are willing to use the court process to get an order enforcing their rights. Fashion brands may seek to restrict the sale of counterfeit handbags, clothing, shoes, or accessories sold in flea

---

10. *See e.g.*, Forum Code of Procedure for IP Disputes Rule 4.4; *see also* Amer. Arb. Ass'n R-38.

markets or online—not because each counterfeit sale is a lost actual sale, but because access to luxury goods must be limited in order for them to maintain their value. A consumer who may actually make such a purchase could see a poor quality counterfeit and be confused as to the quality of the authentic merchandise.

As always, consideration of the facts of a dispute, the relationship of the parties (and any desire to maintain that relationship), the remedies sought, and the timing of the proceeding should all weigh into a prudently informed decision regarding whether to use some form of ADR in lieu of, or together with, litigation.

Copyright Disputes

Copyright disputes are highly factual. Because independent creation[11] is a defense, many copyright law disputes turn on the evaluation of specific tests, such as the abstraction-filtration-comparison test[12] or the extrinsic/intrinsic similarity test.[13] Software copyright disputes can be particularly complex, with issues of employment agreements and trade secrets (developers taking code or knowledge with them), and questions of access to code. Additionally, recent developments in the law regarding open-source code and API code can create questions that turn on the difference between copyright infringement and mere interoperability. Once again, neutrals with specific technological experience can help sort out the issues. Parties may have greater confidence in the decision of a neutral selected by them rather than by a randomly selected jury, particularly where parties are not located in a federal circuit where the courts have a lot of experience with copyright disputes.

Practical Considerations

The practical considerations for copyright are essentially the same as those for trademarks. Parties frequently want, or need, an injunction quickly, and the ability to use the court's contempt powers to aid in the

---

11. The copyright scholar William Patry discusses this long-standing principle in his blog at: http://williampatry.blogspot.com/2005/06/independent-creation-bulwark-of.html (last visited November 12, 2015).

12. As set out by the Second Circuit in Computer Associates International, Inc. v. Altai, Inc., 982 F.2d 693 (2d Cir. 1992).

13. As set out by the Ninth Circuit in Sid & Marty Krofft Television Prods., Inc. v. McDonald's Corp., 562 F.2d 1157 (9th Cir. 1977).

cessation of the infringing activity and turnover or seizure of infringing materials.

As already recognized, arbitration decisions are final and not subject
to any real appellate review. This would effectively waive the ability to
assert novel theories or defenses, and the courts are frequently tinkering
around the edges of fair use, gray market goods, and the first sale doctrine.[14] Having these issues determined by an arbitration panel without
an avenue of appeal could well change the outcome of the case had the
appellate process been available.

Trade Secret Disputes

Trade secret disputes often arise in the context of another dispute: An
inventor disclosing pre-patent work, an employee taking a customer list
or business practice (or in the case of copyright, computer code), or a
franchisee or licensee disclosing a secret recipe or formula. While swift
injunctions can be useful in a trade secret dispute (and are available in
arbitration), often the proverbial horse has left the barn and all that's left
is the calculation of damages. This calculation can be highly technical;
expert neutrals in trademark law, or the specific technical field at issue,
could increase party confidence in the outcome.

Additionally, there may be significant incentives to keeping the
dispute itself, and any documents surrounding it, confidential. Mediation is inherently confidential and nothing about the process is disclosed
to the public.[15] Certain arbitration rules provide for confidentiality in
arbitration and the parties can always contract for confidentiality if
the chosen rules are silent. Further, ADR processes often include the
option for special hearings regarding the trade secrets themselves that
may be conducted without the arbitrator for the evidentiary (main)
hearing present. The secrets are disclosed only on a need-to-know basis
to special masters who can properly evaluate the nature of the secrets
and issue orders regarding disclosures. Some providers have specific

---

14. Kirtsaeng v. John Wiley & Sons, Inc., 133 S. Ct. 1351 (U.S. 2013) (first sale doctrine); Omega
S.A. v. Costco Wholesale Corp., 776 F.3d 692, 694 (9th Cir. Cal. 2015) (gray market goods); Authors
Guild v. Google, Inc., 2015 U.S. App. LEXIS 17988 (2d Cir. N.Y. Oct. 16, 2015) (fair use).

15. *See* FED. R. EVID. 408.

trade secret rules,[16] but any arbitration clause can build in the required protections.

Practical Considerations

It is important, to the extent possible, to differentiate between actual trade secrets and mere proprietary information. True trade secrets may lose their value if publicly disclosed, and confidentiality is of the utmost importance. Consequently, arbitration may be a preferred method of dispute resolution due to the nature of the confidentiality. However, federal courts and business courts routinely manage cases involving trade secrets and have mechanisms in place to allow documents to be filed under seal. But the burden is on the party wishing to seal the records, and courts look at the facts closely to determine if sealing is warranted.[17]

Another consideration is that trade secrets disputes can appear to a jury to be not much more than a business dispute, often between two companies that appear to have substantial resources. Though there is no empirical data the authors are aware of, anecdotal evidence suggests that jurors who remain in a financially challenging position personally may be leery of awarding large sums of money to a company, which may militate in favor of ADR.

Special Franchise and Employment Dispute Considerations

A common complaint about franchise and employment litigation and arbitration is that the time and expense favor the franchisor or the employer. Crafting an ADR clause that provides for a more equal balance of power will be critical if the clause or award is ever reviewed by

---

16. One author is aware that two providers have specific trade secret provisions in their rules: FORUM (www.adrforum.com/IP) and the World Intellectual Property Organization (http://www.wipo.int/amc/en/arbitration/rules/).

17. *See, e.g.,* Oliner v. Kontrabecki, 745 F.3d 1024, 1026 (9th Cir. 2014) ("[O]ur strong presumption of openness does not permit the routine closing of judicial records to the public. The party seeking to seal any part of a judicial record bears the heavy burden of showing that the material is the kind of information that courts will protect and that disclosure will work a clearly defined and serious injury to the party seeking closure.").

a court. The process designed should be fair enough to merit the trust of both contemplated users.[18] Some considerations can include:

- Allocating the shifting of fees to the franchisor or employer,[19]
- Providing for a limited discovery period[20] and quick time-to-hearing,
- Locating the seat of the arbitration or mediation in a venue close to the employee or franchisee,[21] and
- Considering a documentary hearing, instead of an in-person participatory hearing, which can raise costs and increase the amount of time or overwhelm the less sophisticated party.

Practical Considerations

In both situations involving employees and franchise disputes, precedent and visibility may have more value than confidentiality and efficiency. A practitioner representing a business may consider advising the client, especially one who cannot afford frequent litigation, to consider the value of using a dispute to demonstrate to others who may consider engaging in the same actionable conduct to refrain from doing so. For example, a small business with a salesperson violating a restrictive covenant may want the freedom to bring a court action so the rest of the sales team knows that breaching the covenants has real costs and consequences. In addition, getting a single order that finds the covenants to be enforceable will likewise deter similar behavior.

---

18. The major dispute resolution providers have due process protocols in place to help ensure a balance of power in employment claims. *See, e.g.,* FORUM, http://www.adrforum.com/resources/Employment/Due%20Process%20Protections%202015%20Final.docx; and American Arbitration Association, https://www.adr.org/cs/idcplg?IdcService=GET_FILE&dDocName=ADRSTAGE20 25665&RevisionSelectionMethod=LatestReleased.

19. In fact, most arbitration providers require employers to pay or pre-pay the bulk of the arbitration costs as part of their due process protocols. Arbitrators may allocate fees and costs.

20. In most average-sized arbitration cases, discovery can reasonably be completed in about four to six months.

21. Remember, the location of the hearing does not necessarily determine choice of law; the parties can select a substantive law to apply that does not match the location of the hearing. A neutral will be selected that is familiar with the substantive law jurisdiction selected.

Conclusion

In many if not all instances, foresight can save clients money by protecting their IP assets without the risks, uncertainties, delays, disruptions, and costs of court proceedings. ADR is not ideally suited for every situation between all parties; it is often best implemented in contractual arrangements where the parties mindfully consider and negotiate the possibility of dispute before one arises. When parties to a contract are mindful about their expectations for ADR, the scope of potential disputes, and the desired outcomes, it is likely they will not only be able to save time and money in the long run, but will preserve their relationship as well.

CHAPTER 10

Best Practices in Dispute Resolution in Public Infrastructure Projects

Deborah Bovarnick Mastin

EDITOR'S NOTE: Construction projects—particularly long-term public projects such as airports and highways—have been among the most prominent beneficiaries of the growth of ADR. The building of the Hong Kong airport and the modernization of St. Mary's Hospital—also in Hong Kong—were early examples of an approach that revolutionized the industry. This chapter introduces some of the fundamental precepts.

Alternate dispute resolution options on public infrastructure projects are intended to enhance communication among the project team members, to mitigate or avoid disputes arising from claims, and to achieve a speedy binding resolution to disputes that are intractable. Few projects are as large as public infrastructure projects, which in recent years have included dams, airport runways, airside improvements and terminal building construction, seaport facilities, public transit extensions, tunnels, bridges, highways, water, and wastewater systems, hospitals, college classrooms and dormitories, and performing arts centers. Infrastructure projects often involve significant costs, large carrying charges, and impressive overhead commitments by the construction managers and contractors involved in the installation of the project. The cost of unplanned delays caused by the need to procure and install additional components in a multi-million dollar infrastructure project can easily outstrip the direct cost of the components themselves.

For more than five decades, participants in public infrastructure projects have implemented a variety of project delivery systems and project management protocols in an effort to enhance the outcomes of these large complex projects, in the hope of reducing the amount of time and resources diverted to conflict and dispute resolution activities from more productive construction tasks. These project structures and protocols encompass design-build projects, design-build-operate-maintain projects, partnering, standing project neutrals, project adjudication, dispute resolution boards, mediation, and arbitration. A goal shared by all these structures and protocols is to allow the project owner, designer, and constructor an opportunity to address the unplanned circumstances that befall these projects in "real time," while they are underway.

Alternate dispute resolution options are as attractive and as commonplace in public contracts as they are in privately owned and funded projects. Public owners who embark on large infrastructure projects are keenly aware that litigation is costly and time-consuming, and offers no certain or immediate results. However, public owners' construction administration staff will possess varying degrees of familiarity, experience, and comfort levels with alternate dispute resolution options. Some public owners require and identify specific alternate dispute mechanisms in their solicitation packages, while other public owners may need to be introduced to alternate dispute resolution options by their bidders.

Matching ADR Options to Clients' Objectives

Infrastructure projects are intended to improve the quality of life for the local community. They are planned and financed with the best of intentions and the greatest optimism, and they involve significant commitments of public funds and resources. Not wanting to plan for failure and therefore reluctant to plan for risk, public owners rarely include the costs of litigating claims in their project budgets. In public infrastructure projects, it is often the case that the longer a dispute lingers, the more costly the process for resolving that dispute becomes. Including a robust alternate dispute resolution structure in the project specifications allows the parties to better manage their expenses of investigation, the cost of loss of use of unpaid funds, and the other delay costs that accrue while claims resolution processes are extended.

A satisfactory and effective alternate dispute resolution process should be perceived by the parties as cheap, quick, and effective rather than expensive, cumbersome, and redundant. During the negotiations of the project documents, a proposed alternate dispute resolution process may be challenged as a project cost that diminishes the owner's budget for physical enhancements to the project or the designer or constructor's profit margin by increasing its overhead costs. However, these costs are insignificant when compared to the costs of litigating unresolved disputes after the completion of a project.[1]

Using ADR to Meet the Project's Priorities: Predictable Time, Cost, and Quality

When considering whether to include arbitration, mediation, dispute boards, facilitation, or some other ADR structure in the contract documents, parties to prospective infrastructure projects should evaluate each option based on the qualities they seek to obtain and the specific conditions of each project. It is an old saw that each construction project has three elements: quality, time, and cost, which compete for priority as the project proceeds.

With regard to the project's quality, the public owner expects, at a minimum, a completed project that satisfies the owner's intended functional requirements, and hopes the project will display a look and level of finish detail that will make the public agency officials proud of the project. The owner does not want to be disappointed regarding the function, fit, or finish of the finished project, whether the project is a museum, courthouse, tunnel, bridge, dam, highway, airport, seaport, or water management system. The public owner will not likely tolerate a finished project that fails to perform its intended function.

With regard to time, the public owner expects to finish the project on time without the need to pay for additional project management team effort, without the need to move its operations into temporary facilities or to extend existing leases beyond their current termination dates, without the loss of anticipated revenue from a delayed opening of a new facility, and without the need to pay staff who cannot function

---

1. *See*, Carol C. Menassa and Feniosky Peña Mora, *Analysis of Dispute Review Boards Application in U.S. Construction Projects from 1975 to 2007*, J. OF MGMT. IN ENG'G (April 2010).

in their intended job functions because the facility is not ready for use on time.

Because the funding for infrastructure projects is generally defined by bond proceeds or by grant awards and is therefore fixed at a maximum amount, the public owner will seek to maintain its project costs within the available funding. The public owner will generally prefer that a project's claims and delays be minimized and that the cost of its dispute resolution process be planned and controlled. The public owner attempts to keep the cost of the project within its budgeted funds and hopes to avoid escalating labor or material costs or other unforeseen complications that will cause budgeted funds to be inadequate to finish the project. Unbudgeted expenses are unwelcome.

When undertaking a significant infrastructure project, a public owner generally prefers budget predictability to risk. While the public owner understands that lower risk comes at a higher cost, the public owner may prefer a balance favoring certainty. This is because (1) construction work is not its core business activity and it feels less competent evaluating the risks associated with the construction than it does with its core business operations of providing public services, and (2) when its project budget is fixed, it has no ready source for additional funding.

It is inevitable that unplanned events will occur during the progress of a large and complex project, and so the alternate dispute resolution provisions in the contract documents should provide a roadmap for responding to these anticipated but unplanned events in a way that minimizes both the impact on the project and the administrative cost of the response process. To mitigate adverse impacts on the project in the event the project team does not see eye-to-eye on the requirements in a particular instance, the contract documents for an infrastructure project may require a meeting of project executives, a partnering plan, the implementation of a dispute board, a standing project neutral, a mediator, or arbitration or litigation. Failure to include a contractual mechanism for responding to unplanned events can be costly; precious time may be consumed while the parties come to agreement on a response mechanism before they can initiate that response mechanism to assess an appropriate response, and the project will have moved away from orderly progression towards chaos.

The Means to the End—Communications and Civility

Civility and open communications on the project among the various members of the infrastructure project team, the designer, the contractor and the owner's staff, will enhance the likelihood of meeting the primary objectives of quality, time, and budget. New projects are fun and exciting; at the start of a new project, everyone involved is optimistic about the project. However, if expectations of any party are not being met during the progress of the work, resentment may build between the parties. Unchecked resentment will lead to lack of quality performance, delays, and cost escalations. Structured opportunities for open communication can minimize the likelihood of the development of a hostile environment on the job site. No owner wants its project to be the one that everyone hates being on, simply because the attitudes on site are irritating.

Several means are commonly used on large construction projects to enhance communications among the party members. Three common methods intended to enhance communications and minimize disputes are "the big room" (also referred to as "co-location"), partnering, and Dispute Boards. If available space permits, the practice of "co-location," physically placing the design and construction team members in the same office space, is a simple but effective means of supporting frequent communications among the project team. Partnering meetings are another means of enhancing communications, making decisions that affect the project at the lowest level of staff authority, and elevating unresolved decisions to project executives.

The third approach involves the early and consistent implementation of a proactive dispute board that meets regularly with the express purpose of avoiding disputes, minimizing impacts to the project from unplanned events, and facilitating a collaborative response to the unexpected.

After claims have been asserted, a standing neutral or project mediator can help the parties resolve responsibility for problems that have already occurred, prior to initiating any litigation or arbitration proceedings.

Frosting on the Cake—Enhancing Business Relationships

This project may not be the only project the public owner plans to undertake over the next few years, and the public owner hopes to work with exemplary contractors for each project. Initiating a public project often requires that a unique procurement package be planned and drafted, and the proposals received in response to the solicitation invitation need to be individually evaluated and ranked. Each step in the public agency's process of identifying satisfactory business partners is a high-risk and stressful effort, involving a significant commitment of the agency's staff time and resources. If the public agency's relationships with the design and construction teams it has previously engaged are satisfactory and stress-free, then it will be interested in engaging them again for other projects.

In the private sector, if an owner's expectations of quality, schedule, and cost are met, and if the job site is a collaborative and professional work environment, the owner is likely to choose to work with the team again and again. In public sector work, procurements are moving towards more "qualifications-based" selection, rather than the simpler lowest price procurement model of design-bid-build. This trend in procurement methods aligns the public agency's expectations with those of a private owner when selecting its business partners. In evaluating a designer or a contractor for future work, a public owner would likely consider criteria such as:

(i)   whether the owner's expectations of time, cost, and quality were met, disappointed, or exceeded;

(ii) whether unplanned events were handled efficiently or even creatively;

(iii) whether the contractor or designer's staff is congenial to work with or whether the relationship imposed an administrative burden on the owner's staff; and

(iv) whether the contractor or designer made the owner's staff look competent or whether they seemed unable to control the project.

The contractor or consultant's skills in these areas of project administration may well color the evaluation of its proposals for future work with the public agency.

Evaluating the Merits or Effectiveness of an Alternate Dispute Resolution Process in a Solicitation Package

The public owner places a high priority on minimizing the administrative process cost of its infrastructure project and of the dispute resolution mechanisms that arise from the project. The public owner would prefer to spend that money on enhancements to the project, so every dollar spent on process represents a lost opportunity for a better project.

Rather than engage in a litigation process of uncertain cost, duration, and outcome, a public owner may prefer an alternate dispute resolution process that will allow it to manage and predict the cost and time of the process and to maintain some control over the outcome, or at least over the selection of the decision makers. Mediation is an attractive ADR process for public infrastructure projects because the parties retain at least partial control over the cost and time of the process, the process cost is modest, and the outcome could be final. Further, the parties retain significant control over the outcome, and they cannot be forced to accept an unattractive agreement. Arbitration offers the advantage of some reduction of process cost and time as compared with litigation. Also, the ability to have a voice in the selection of the decision-maker is attractive, and the confidentiality of the proceeding may also be attractive; on the other hand, a public owner may prefer to establish a precedent for other future similar projects, which would enhance the predictability of the arbitration outcome for those projects.

ADR options during project performance for dispute mitigation and Avoidance

In crafting the documents that create the project structure—the contract with the designer, the contract with the contractor, and the contracts for other supporting members of the project team—various mechanisms are commonly implemented in order to maximize opportunities to mitigate and to avoid claims and disputes. Two common mechanisms used in infrastructure projects are partnering and Dispute Boards.

Partnering and Facilitation

Partnering has a long history of use in the construction industry. A partnering protocol will generally require the parties to communicate in a professional and civil manner regarding the project events, from the outset of the planning period and well before the ground is broken. With working relationships well established, partnering often attempts to empower the field personnel to arrive at decisions about the project and to involve supervisors or project executives only when the field staff is unable to reach consensus. If consensus cannot be reached by the parties working alone, a facilitator may be invited to monitor the communications between parties with the goal of achieving agreement. While partnering appears to offer the lowest cost of all alternate dispute methods, anecdotal evidence shared by owners indicates that many partnering endeavors are ineffective as implemented. While some public agencies still require contractors to enter into partnering agreements as a condition of the construction contract,[2] in my experience, the former readiness of owners to mandate partnering protocols in the contracts is on the wane[3] because partnering does not reliably provide a satisfactory forum for resolving disputes that arise during the progress of the work.

Dispute Resolution Boards

Dispute Resolution Boards (also called Dispute Review Boards, Dispute Boards, or Dispute Avoidance Panels, all referred to here as "Dispute Boards") can be crafted to operate in a variety of modalities, from proactive facilitative Dispute Boards, to Dispute Adjudication Boards, which are a form of expedited arbitration panels selected before any disputes arise, but called into operation only after the submission of a formal claim. A typical Dispute Board is composed of three impartial and neutral industry experts, selected for their personal experience with the particular type of project and for their alternate dispute resolution experience. While more expensive than a partnering facilitator because of the number of panelists and the regular frequency of their meetings,

---

2. *See, e.g.*, CAL. DEP'T TRANSP., FIELD GUIDE TO PARTNERING ON CALTRANS CONSTRUCTION PROJECTS, (www.dot.ca.gov); Colo. Dep't Transp. (www.codot.gov); Minn. Dep't Transp. (www.state.mn.us); Nev. Dep't Transp. (www.nevadadot.com).

3. *See*, "The Truth about Partnering, Limitations and Solutions," 21(2) AAA PUNCH LIST, August 1998; ADR CONSTRUCTION, ABA 2014 (www.constructionadrbook.com).

proactive Dispute Boards offer the benefits of collaborative facilitation during the progress of the work and can convert to non-binding or binding arbitration if consensus is not reached between the parties. On smaller projects, such as those under $10 million, it may be more cost effective to use a single-person Dispute Board or to limit the Dispute Board's regular meetings to a half day.

A significant body of anecdotal evidence, as well as industry studies,[4] indicate that pro-active Dispute Boards effectively facilitate project progress and minimize cost increases while maintaining relationships on the job. The database of the Dispute Resolution Board Foundation identifies over 40 various public agencies in the United States, including state departments of transportation, water and wastewater districts, and port and airport authorities, that have utilized Dispute Boards on their infrastructure projects within the last ten years, in addition to a significant number of international infrastructure projects with Dispute Boards.[5]

Dispute Boards are created by the contract between the owner and the contractor. The most effective manner of implementation of the Dispute Board is to require the parties to discuss current ongoing project events at Dispute Board meetings and to allow the parties a forum for ameliorating the impact of events that have not yet occurred. To be effective, these discussions should occur prior to "stepped" decision making, with no preconditions to involvement (such as an owner's rejection of a request for additional compensation), and prior to any formal mediation between the parties.

The Dispute Board should meet at regularly scheduled intervals, especially in the absence of any presented claim, the primary purpose being to allow the Dispute Board panel the opportunity to facilitate the way the parties respond to future events on the project rather than argue about who is responsible for events that already occurred and expenses already incurred. In several areas of the country, it is the custom for the owner to pay the entire cost of regular meetings, but in other areas, another common cost allocation protocol is used, which is to assess the owner and the contractor each half of the cost of the regular meetings.

---

4. See CAROL C. MENASSA AND FENIOSKY PENA MORA, ANALYSIS OF DISPUTE REVIEW BOARDS APPLICATION IN U.S. CONSTRUCTION PROJECTS FROM 1975 TO 2007, http://www.asce/library.org; See also RALPH ELLIS, DISPUTE REVIEW BOARD & PROJECT DISPUTES FLORIDA DEPARTMENT OF TRANSPORTATION, http://www.dot.state.fl.us/structures/DesignConf2006/Presentations/Session6/Final-6Ellis.pdf (downloaded July 16, 2013).

5. Dispute Resolution Board Foundation (www.drb.org).

It can be in the owner's interest to pay the entire cost of these regular meetings directly, both because the cost will be included within the contractor's fee and ultimately paid by the owner in any event, and also to be better able to resist pressure to skip or cancel regularly scheduled Dispute Board meetings. Generally, the cost of formal dispute hearings, should there be any, will be shared by the parties. Many projects with Dispute Boards reach completion without the need to convene any dispute hearings at all during the progress of the work and without any arbitration or litigation after the project has been accepted by the public owner.

Dispute Boards may offer informal, non-written guidance opinions that can color future negotiations between the parties. Involving a mediator prior to consideration of an issue by the Dispute Board has not been found to be effective and further delays the Dispute Board's consideration of a disputed matter. If the parties cannot reach agreement with the assistance of the informal guidance, the Dispute Board can convene a formal dispute hearing to consider the dispute and will issue a written recommendation to the parties. After the Dispute Board has rendered a formal or an informal recommendation as to entitlement, a mediator may be engaged to expeditiously assist the parties in resolving any outstanding issues of valuation.

Proactive Dispute Boards are a prudent investment on infrastructure projects because they effectively encourage creative and timely solutions from the project team in response to the unplanned events that occur on construction projects, and at a minimum cost. Dispute Boards are also particularly helpful in assisting the parties in maintaining cordial professional relationships during the progress of the work. Template specifications for Dispute Boards are available from a number of sources.[6]

Standing Neutral

Another means of addressing disputes while a project is ongoing is to engage a "Standing Neutral," essentially a qualified neutral mediator, who is selected by the parties at the commencement of a project to

---

6. *See, e.g.,* Dispute Resolution Board Foundation (www.drb.org); ConsensusDocs, DRB Addendum Documents 200.4 and 200.5 (www.consensusdocs.org); International Institute for Conflict Prevention & Resolution (www.cpradr.org); International Chamber of Commerce (www.iccwbo.org).

be available on an as-needed basis to help the parties resolve disputes as they arise during the progress of the work. This structure offers the advantage of a trained mediator who is familiar with the project and the parties and does not need to be introduced to the underlying situation on the project with each new issue that arises. The intention is to avoid large omnibus claims that linger until the conclusion of the project. Use of a standing neutral can also ameliorate the accumulation of hostility between the parties that so often accompanies unresolved disputes on a project. This is another effective ADR tool that owners often adopt to promote continuity and harmony on the project. As the standing neutral is only utilized when a dispute arises, the process cost is minimized, and both parties retain all the control of the outcome offered by a mediation. Because the disputes are addressed individually, the preparation time for staff is significantly less as compared to a mediation process that commenced after project completion when a series of disputes had accumulated.

Dispute Adjudication Board

Unlike a proactive dispute review board, which focuses on mitigation and avoidance of claims, a dispute adjudication board is essentially a pre-selected arbitration panel. The single adjudicator or Dispute Adjudication Board is intended to provide expedited adjudication of individual disputes when they arise during the progress of the project. Expedited adjudication is mandated by statute in the United Kingdom[7] and has found a high user satisfaction there, but has not been widely adopted in the United States. Typically, the decision of the adjudicator as to entitlement is binding on the parties during the progress of the work, but is subject to judicial review at the completion of the project. The adjudication structure prevents an owner from unreasonably refusing to pay the contractor for changes to the work, or for additional cost to perform the work that it has authorized or for which it is legally responsible. Even if the owner challenges the adjudicator's determination, the owner is bound to follow that determination and to pay for the disputed work during the progress of the project, until the adjudicator's determination is judicially overturned on review.

---

7. Housing Grants, Construction and Regeneration Act 1996, http://www.legislation.gov.uk/ukpga/1996/53/contents.

Mediation: Pre-suit and Pre-trial

If disputes have not been adequately avoided or mitigated during the progress of the work but linger after the completion of the project, resolution of disputes with the assistance of a skilled mediator who specializes in construction disputes is an attractive option. The cost of a mediator is relatively small, compared to the cost of the construction dispute, and a skilled mediator can provide a safe forum for the disputing parties to come to a mutually acceptable accord. A mediator can soften emotional barriers that have impeded successful negotiations between the parties, and a creative mediator can also suggest solutions that would not be available to the parties in an arbitration or litigation case, such as agreements regarding future work, or contributing services or labor towards remedying an unsatisfactory outcome rather than simply paying money. The confidential nature of mediation proceedings and of mediated settlement agreements is an additional advantage that may be attractive to the parties. Further, mediation offers the potential of the speediest final resolution of a dispute, as compared to arbitration and litigation proceedings, and appellate proceedings.

The ability to craft resolutions that include non-monetary considerations or considerations outside the direct parameters of the dispute at issue may also be an advantage of the mediation process; for example, the promise of future work or the reversal of a default may motivate a settlement. These components of an ultimate solution would not be available to the parties in arbitration or in litigation.

Pre-suit mediation does have inherent limitations. First of all, by the time the parties agree to mediate, the defect, impact, or damage has already occurred. Mediation does not often offer any opportunity for the parties to mitigate the extent of the defect, impact, or damage, but can only allocate responsibility and cost for the remediation.

In order to maximize the opportunity for a successful mediation, even before any suit is filed, each party can take steps to improve the likelihood of achieving a satisfactory outcome. Early in the mediation process, parties should fully investigate the facts and conclusions involved in the dispute, paying particular attention to the claimed and documented cost of the disputed work. The ultimate decision makers need sufficient reliable information to enable them to make a reasoned settlement in the mediation.

The mediation process begins long before the mediation conference: The parties each need to assign a staff representative with full authority to resolve the disputed matter, and that person needs to become immersed in the details of the dispute, both as presented by the owner's staff and as described by the claimant. Rather than rely on the assigned project staff, the decision makers need to make the time available to attend the entire mediation hearing. Prior arrangements should be made so the decision makers have immediate access, either in person or by phone, to those staff or consultants who can provide in-depth resource material and verification of disputed points. Often, the field staff who made the initial determinations are too rooted in their established view of entitlement to make a rational business decision. If one party elevates the authority level of its representative at the mediation, the other party can usually be persuaded to select a higher-ranking representative as well. A commitment from both sides to bring the highest-level executive needed with full authority to satisfy or abandon the full demand can be helpful in resolving a dispute in mediation. Similarly, one or more of the parties may consider engaging special "settlement counsel," separate from its outside litigation counsel, to assist in the mediation process. The practice of utilizing settlement counsel frees the litigation counsel to focus on the factual and legal requirements of the trial or arbitration, while the settlement counsel incorporates the client's business concerns into its objectives for a satisfactory outcome in mediation.

The growing practice of "early mediation" (also sometimes known as "Guided Choice"[8]) allows the mediator to help structure exchanges of information between the parties that are narrowly tailored to furnishing data that the decision makers on each side need in order to evaluate their respective positions. A claimant who provides complete documentation of its claims to an owner in mediation better validates its claims and can better convince a skeptical owner of the merits and value of the claim. Similarly, an owner who furnishes the claimant in advance of the mediation conference with documentary support for its reluctance to acknowledge the claim or the amount of the claim may more persuasively motivate the claimant to reevaluate the value of its demands. Providing documentation sufficiently in advance of the mediation so that the opposing party's internal staff and consultants can study and evaluate the information is a far more effective mediation strategy than springing records at the mediation conference.

---

8. Paul M. Lurie, *Guided Choice Arbitration*, 11 DePaul Bus. & Com. L.J. 455 (2013), available at: http://via.library.depaul.edu/bclj/vol11/iss4/3; Paul M. Lurie, *Guided Choice: Early Mediated Settlements and/or Customized Arbitrations*, 7 J. Amer. C. Constr. Law. 167 (2013).

Arbitration

The United States and local jurisdictions have long expressed strong public policy support for arbitration of commercial disputes and in particular in connection with commercial disputes involving the federal government.[9]

Arbitration is a creature of contract, and arbitration agreements can be crafted across a full spectrum of alternative dispute resolution processes. Arbitration that merely replicates litigation, except with a panel of three paid arbitrators in place of a judge, squanders the promise of a quicker, cheaper, and more satisfactory process. Unconstrained discovery in arbitration can be just as costly as litigation.

Generally, the elements of arbitration that are attractive to infrastructure project participants include (1) the parties' control over the selection of the panel, along with confidence that the panel will be knowledgeable about construction practices and contract interpretation, as well as neutral and attentive; (2) speed of resolution; (3) limitations on joinder and discovery, leading to a simpler and less costly process as compared with litigation, and often; (4) confidentiality of the proceedings. Parties' selection of the panel members may contribute to an enhanced sense of a fair hearing and to a greater satisfaction with process, as compared with litigation, where a judge may have little prior experience with complex construction matters. The confidentiality of an arbitration process may be an advantage or a disadvantage, depending on the circumstances. If the outcome of a dispute may have value as precedent for other pending or potentially pending disputes of a similar nature, a party may prefer to have the determination available in the public record.

In the past, some parties have been reluctant to agree to arbitrate disputes having high value because of the limited grounds for challenging a disappointing arbitration decision under the Federal Arbitration Act or under state law. To address that concern, the major domestic alternate dispute resolution providers[10] now offer ancillary appellate arbitration rules and procedures that the parties may select.

---

9. The Federal Arbitration Act, 9 U.S.C. §§ 1 *et seq.*, authorizes arbitration as a voluntary means of dispute resolution in public and in private disputes. Title 5 U.S.C. Subchapter 4, Sections 571 *et seq.*, Alternative Means of Dispute Resolution in the Administrative Process, authorizes federal agencies to engage in dispute resolution outside of the court system and encourages each agency to establish its own appropriate dispute resolution procedures.

10. American Arbitration Association (www.adr.org); JAMS (www.jamsadr.com); International Institute for Conflict Prevention & Resolution (www.cpradr.org).

In drafting an arbitration agreement, the parties need to consider their preferences for a satisfactory process. The choice of venue, choice of applicable law, choice of applicable arbitration administration and rules, and agreements as to discovery protocols all deserve evaluation, and each can impact the parties' ultimate satisfaction with the fairness of the outcome.

Anticipating the special demands of an arbitration process will allow the parties to optimize the benefits of the process. The scheduling of submission deadlines in an arbitration proceeding will likely be accelerated, compared to litigation time frames. Early engagement of counsel with arbitration experience, not just litigation experience, is helpful to parties seeking to achieve an efficient resolution in arbitration. Engagement of technical consultants before commencing an arbitration process is not only more cost-effective than pushing a consultant to expedite an investigation and a report, but can also serve as a form of early case evaluation for the parties.

It is crucial that, from the earliest stages of an arbitration, each party focus on the evidence that supports the claimed damages as well as the grounds for claimed liability.

Each party will want access to those project records that bear upon the actual cost of the work or any portion of it so that it need not rely only on estimates prepared by its staff and consultants. Each party's ability to perform an accurate risk assessment of its exposures and potential recovery in the arbitration depends in large part upon the quality of information available to the decision makers within the party's internal corporate structure.

Non-binding Arbitration

Even when a dispute will be resolved by trial in court, alternate dispute resolution options can help minimize the risks and process costs of litigation in high-risk, high-dollar disputes that are commonly seen after the completion of infrastructure projects. Convening a non-binding arbitration prior to trial, either by court order or by agreement of the parties, can offer the parties an opportunity to avoid a potentially shocking result in trial. The procedures for the non-binding arbitration could be established by court order or may be agreed to between the parties. The process may be submission of trial briefs, certain evidence, and argument of counsel, without any live testimony or with only limited live testimony. In some jurisdictions, if the disappointed party does not accept the recommendation of the arbitrator and elects to proceed to trial, then costs and attorneys' fees will shift to that party if the ultimate recovery does not exceed an established threshold.[11]

Settlement Issues with an Owner Who Is a Public Agency

Sovereign Immunity: Authority to Settle and to Approve Changes in the Work

In many local jurisdictions, the public employees who are managing the project for the public owner (and even more so, the consultants who have been engaged to perform project management services) do not have inherent, or apparent, authority to bind the public entity or to compromise or to settle a claim asserted either by or against the public agency[12] because the public owner is, in fact, the elected body of the public entity, and not its various employees. The authority of those public employees is limited by applicable legal constraints. It is essential that counsel for parties contracting with local government entities be familiar with the limits of the authority of the public staff with regards to the specific contract at issue.

If not expressly provided in the project contract documents, it may be possible, after a dispute has arisen, to seek an express delegation of authority from the elected body to a specifically designated public employee to pursue settlement negotiations within defined limits or to compromise the public entity's position on an issue. Otherwise, no

---

11. *See, e.g.,* 103 Fla. Stat. § 44. Alternatively, in the absence of express statutory authorization, an arbitration agreement can be drafted to incorporate the concepts embodied in Fed. R. Civ. P. 68 to shift costs incurred by a party tendering an offer of judgment subsequent to the rejection of the offer, if the awarded amount is less favorable than the offer.

12. In Florida, while employees of the State of Florida have the authority to compromise or settle claims without going to the Florida Legislature for express authority on each matter, employees of counties, municipalities, school districts, and other local government agencies do not have that authority. *See,* 125 Fla. Stat. and Fla. Const. art. 8 § 1 (counties); 166 Fla Stat. and Fla. Const. art. 8 § 2 (municipalities); 235 Fla. Stat. (school boards); Frankenmuth Mutual Insurance Co. v. Magaha, 769 So.2d 1012 (Fla. 2002). Unless the contract contains an express delegation of authority to the local government staff, whether the City Manager or the Director of the Department of General Services, local government employees only have the power to recommend change orders or to recommend settlement agreements to the elected body of government officials.

settlement agreement will be binding on the public entity until it is approved or ratified by the elected body that awarded the contract.

Prohibition Against Use of Public Funds to Benefit Private Entities

Public entities may only enter into contracts and spend public funds on activities that result in a public purpose.[13] The enabling constitutions, charters, or legislation of many jurisdictions contain prohibitions against or limitations on use of public funds to benefit private entities.[14] In order to comply with those legal limitations, a public owner's ability to compromise or to settle a claim must demonstrate mutual consideration; in other words, the public entity must receive something of value in return for its offer to pay or to compromise.

Limits on Confidentiality of Settlement Terms

In jurisdictions that have enacted Public Records statutes, or local Freedom of Information acts,[15] it may not possible to shield the terms of a settlement agreement from public view and inspection. The public's (and the public media's) right to have access to commercial transactions may transcend any considerations of private convenience by the contracting parties.[16] While the settlement negotiations themselves may remain confidential, the ultimate settlement document is likely to be required to be disclosed to public review.

Non-disparagement Clauses

While it is common in private settlement agreements to include covenants that neither party will discuss the terms of the settlement or that the parties agree not to disparage each other, such provisions may not be possible when one of the parties is a public agency. Many jurisdictions

---

13. Loan Association v. Topeka, 87 U.S. (20 Wall.) 655 (1874).

14. *See, e.g.,* FLA. CONST. art. 8 § 10 ("Section 10. Pledging credit. Neither the state nor any county, school district, municipality, special district, or agency of any of them, shall become a joint owner with, or stockholder of, or give, lend or use its taxing power or credit to aid any corporation, association, partnership or person…" subject to exceptions listed.).

15. *See, e.g.,* Florida Public Records Act, 119 FLA. STAT.; California Public Records Act, CAL. GOV'T. CODE §§ 6250–6270; New York Freedom of Information Law, N.Y. PUB. OFF. §§ 84–90.

16. For example, Florida Public Records Act, 119 FLA. STAT., contains certain specific exemptions and exclusions from the general requirement that public records are to be made available for inspection and copying. *See* 119 FLA. STAT. §§ 119.0701, 119.1171–1714.

have enacted codes of conduct for public officials and employees or have included a citizen's right to accurate information in response to a question as part of a local citizens' bill of rights.[17] These legislative requirements would likely preclude enforcement of a provision in a settlement agreement that purportedly prevented a public agency or its officials or employees from making truthful, but disparaging, statements about a contractor or its performance. Other jurisdictions may have adopted an internal procedure that prohibits the public employees from entering into agreements that contain anti-disparagement provisions.

Converting a Termination for Default into a Termination for Convenience

A valuable settlement option in mediation is the opportunity for the parties to agree to convert a previously issued Termination for Default into a Termination for Convenience, in return for concessions by the contractor that are acceptable to the public owner. Because it is common for public agencies to demand disclosure of past defaults from those bidding on new public work and to evaluate the qualifications of potential contractors and consultants using this data, it is particularly valuable to those who perform public work on a recurring basis to have the ability to negotiate a reversal of a default determination.

Agreement Not to Bid on Future Agency Project

Contractors and consultants engaged in a particularly unpleasant dispute on an infrastructure project may obtain resolution of that dispute during mediation or another alternate dispute resolution process by voluntarily agreeing to refrain from seeking to obtain future contract work from that public agency. If, however, that agreement is deemed to be a debarment, that debarment may have to be disclosed when responding to solicitations issued by other public agencies for new work and may adversely affect the agencies' evaluation of that debarred bidder's qualifications for the new work.

---

17. *See, e.g.,* Miami-Dade County, Florida, Citizens' Bill of Rights ("Truth in Government. No County or municipal official or employee shall knowingly furnish false information on any public matter, nor knowingly omit significant facts when giving requested information to members of the public.") Section A (2), Miami-Dade County Charter, http://ethics.miamidade.gov/library/Publications/citizens_bill_of_rights.pdf.

Direct Communications with Public Officials by Opposing Counsel

Local statutes, ordinances, and professional codes of conduct may limit direct communications by counsel for a design professional or a constructor with the public officials who are managing the infrastructure project. While some local ethics rules expressly permit direct communication with public officials even though public agency is represented by in-house or outside counsel,[18] this position is not universal.[19] When involved in a public infrastructure project, the parties should be aware of the limits on acceptable communications in the particular jurisdiction of the project. Communications with the public agency's attorneys, both in-house and outside counsel, is a prudent precaution.

False Claims, Criminal Liability, License Revocation, Debarment

A contractor embroiled in a dispute on an infrastructure project may face exposure to risks beyond contract damages to the public owner or the contractor's failure to realize its anticipated profit. Following the enactment of the federal False Claims Act,[20] many state and local jurisdictions have also enacted False Claims statutes that impose sanctions, including treble damages, for claims asserted against the public agency that are found to be false or inflated.[21] In addition to damages for breach of contract, a successful claim by a public agency that its contractor or designer presented false or inflated claims may expose the contractor or designer to potential administrative, civil, or criminal sanctions. The public entity may seek to prevent the contractor or designer from competing for future work from the entity in a debarment proceeding, or the licensing board may seek to suspend or to revoke the authorization it had issued to the contractor or designer. The applicable False Claims Act may also

---

18. *See, e.g.*, CAL. RULES PROF'L CONDUCT R.2-100 C(1) (Communication with a Represented Party).

19. *See, e.g.*, FLA. RULES PROF'L CONDUCT R.4-4.2 (Communications with Person Represented by Counsel).

20. False Claims Act, 31 U.S.C. §§ 3729–3733.

21. *See, e.g.*, Florida False Claims Act, FLA. STAT. §§ 68.081 *et seq.*

provide for a private cause of action should the public agency elect not to pursue false claims against its contractor or consultant.

Crafting an alternate dispute resolution structure that encompasses these exposures may be difficult or impossible because each of these potential sanctions may be governed by its own statutory or regulatory procedure,[22] and the public official or body who controls the construction of the infrastructure project may not have control over a debarment, license revocation, or criminal prosecution proceeding. While it may not be feasible to consolidate these disparate exposures in a single arbitration brought to remedy a claimed breach of contract, it may, however, be possible to resolve distinct and disparate exposures pending in separate proceedings as part of a global mediated settlement. The willingness of the affected public agencies to engage in these discussions should be explored.

Conclusion

Public infrastructure projects are enormously complex undertakings involving numerous participants and extensive commitment of resources that offer the project team members the opportunity to enhance the quality of life for a generation of users. In order to optimize the potential for these projects to be completed on time and within budget, the contract documents often include alternate dispute resolution provisions that set out structures to support communication channels on the job site and that establish clear roadmaps for timely responses to the unplanned events that may befall these projects.

Counsel who are knowledgeable about the potential benefits and cost savings associated with the full spectrum of alternate dispute resolution options and who can assist with crafting and implementing appropriate alternate dispute resolution protocols on these projects can provide their public owner, professional design firm, and large construction contractor clients with valuable service in connection with their infrastructure projects.

---

22. *See, e.g.*, 2 C.F.R. Part 180.

CHAPTER 11

Arbitration: What It Was and Could Be Again

William J. Nissen and Louis F. Burke, Private Litigation Subcommittee, Derivatives and Futures Law Committee, Business Law Section[1]

EDITOR'S NOTE: One of the ancient attributes of commercial arbitration—dating from the medieval trade guilds—is the master craftsman's serving as judge in a dispute regarding trade practice. Disputants in specific industries often seek resolution of conflicts according to industry practice, not general law applicable to any commercial endeavor. In this chapter, William Nissen and Louis Burke bring us back full circle, to a new innovation that is really quite old.

One of the early forms of arbitration was an industry-specific process where commercial disputes in a particular industry were resolved by arbitrators from that same industry. The arbitrators had no personal stake in the dispute, but knew the customs and practices that were normally followed in that industry. In addition to avoiding the need for formal litigation in general, arbitration with industry arbitrators does not require education of a judge or jury in the customs and practices of the industry. Instead, arbitrators who already know those customs and practices can turn directly to the issues in dispute and can evaluate the evidence and arguments against the background of their specialized knowledge.

---

1. For information on the Derivatives and Futures Law Committee of the ABA Business Law Section, *see* http://apps.americanbar.org/dch/committee.cfm?com=CL620000 (last accessed February 25, 2016).

This type of business-to-business industry arbitration continues to exist in the commodity futures industry, where members of the commodity futures exchanges, such as Chicago Board of Trade, Chicago Mercantile Exchange, New York Mercantile Exchange, and ICE Futures U.S., and the industry-wide self-regulatory organization, National Futures Association ("NFA"), resolve disputes among the members of their respective organizations. This model has preserved many of the attributes of traditional industry arbitration and could perhaps be an example for other industries.

Each exchange has members who have bought or leased trading rights on the exchanges. There are a number of classifications of membership, ranging from members who act as brokers to provide access to the exchange for public customers, to members who trade solely for their own accounts, but do so in large enough volume that it is cost effective to become a member in order to obtain the lower transaction fees that are applicable to members. Reflecting the wide range of futures contracts traded on the exchanges, non-broker members that trade for their own accounts include producers and users of agricultural or other physical commodities, energy companies, firms that deal in financial instruments, and companies that trade for speculative purposes.

NFA members consist of persons who are registered with the federal regulatory agency, the Commodity Futures Trading Commission, to engage in business with public customers. These registered persons include brokers known as futures commission merchants (futures brokers that are permitted to hold customer funds) and introducing brokers (futures brokers that are not permitted to hold customer funds); commodity trading advisors that trade on behalf of public customers on a discretionary basis; and commodity pool operators that organize and operate collective investment vehicles in which customers can purchase interests in order to participate in investments by those vehicles in commodity futures contracts.

The range of disputes resolved by the exchanges and NFA is wide, reflecting the different types of activities from which disputes may arise. The exchanges, which provide a venue for the execution of trades, tend to resolve disputes relating to the execution of trades. NFA, which covers a broad range of activities by its members (including solicitation of customers and orders and recommendations of trades as well as trade execution), resolves disputes related to this broad range of activities. Each of these organizations also has facilities and rules for arbitration of disputes between members and their customers, but those are handled separately from member-to-member disputes.[2]

It is a condition of membership in an exchange and NFA that the member agrees to arbitrate specified industry-related disputes with other members. Each forum has its own specific rules and procedures, but they have characteristics in common that are distinctive to the industry. These characteristics include: (1) arbitrators who in most cases are not lawyers; (2) limited discovery that is generally restricted to the exchange of documents and information without oral depositions; (3) arbitrators who are members or affiliated with members of the organization and thereby are presumed to have pre-existing industry knowledge; (4) informal hearings chaired by a non-lawyer; and (5) relatively prompt decisions rendered on the basis of a hearing without post-hearing briefing.

Although exchange and NFA arbitration rely much less on lawyers than general commercial arbitration does, lawyers have a role in the process. Exchange and NFA arbitration panels generally have a staff lawyer available from the sponsoring organization to advise the panel during the hearing, as well as in pre-hearing procedures and deliberations. In addition, the parties in these proceedings are generally represented by lawyers who handle pre-hearing proceedings, present and cross-examine witnesses at the hearing, and give opening statements and closing arguments. Thus, legal advice and representation is part of the process, but the actual decision making is handled for the most part by non-lawyers with industry expertise.

The use of non-lawyer arbitrators makes the arbitration proceedings less formal and less legalistic. Non-lawyer arbitrators tend to focus heavily on industry expectations and business relationships, and not as much on the legal relationships, in deciding the cases. Moreover, with the non-lawyer arbitrators having industry expertise, the presentations can be accomplished more quickly and efficiently than a presentation to a judge or jury who is new to the field.

Limited discovery creates substantial economies and efficiencies for member arbitration in the commodity futures industry. The waste

---

2. *See, e.g.,* NFA Member Arbitration Rules, http://www.nfa.futures.org/nfamanual/ NFAManualTOC.aspx?Section=6 and NFA Code of Arbitration (for customer disputes), http:// www.nfa.futures.org/nfamanual/NFAManual.aspx?Section=5.

of time and expense of oral depositions is eliminated. This absence of depositions affects the procedure in a number of respects. Because these arbitrations are often settled prior to hearing (like other arbitrations and litigation), an imminent hearing prompts settlements more quickly and more inexpensively, without the delay and expense of intervening depositions. If the case goes to hearing, the opposing lawyers will both be in the same position of cross-examining adverse witnesses without pre-trial testimony. Apart from saving time and money for the clients, there is a positive side to this for the lawyers, because an unscripted hearing without prior deposition testimony presents a professional challenge that gives the lawyer a greater opportunity to use his or her trial skills.

The informality of the hearings helps arbitrators to get to the essence of the dispute without applying rules of evidence and procedural technicalities. Witness testimony is often presented through a narrative by the witness, without the need for a series of detailed and legally correct questions and potential objections. Arbitrators themselves feel free to ask questions as part of the process, giving them the opportunity to go directly to what they believe they need to know and allowing the parties some insight into what the arbitrators are thinking, so that they can direct their presentations accordingly. An arbitrator's questions, moreover, can benefit the process by the injection of the arbitrator's own industry knowledge and expertise.

Relatively prompt decision making is also a characteristic of commodity futures industry member arbitration. It is not unusual in an exchange arbitration to receive a decision the same day as the hearing. For many disputes, the arbitration will be conducted in a single afternoon, the arbitrators will remain and decide the case after the hearing, and the staff attorney will notify the parties of the decision the same day, with the written decision to follow. Even in more complex arbitrations, where there is more than one day of hearings and the arbitrators meet subsequently to decide the case, there are typically no post-hearing briefs that would delay the decision and increase the costs of the process.

The availability of a staff attorney to advise the panel is an important part of the process. Although non-lawyer panels are capable of conducting fair hearings and rendering awards based on the evidence and industry practices, the attorney-advisor is valuable in ensuring that the hearing and the award meet legal requirements so as to be enforceable if challenged.

In general, the exchange arbitration processes are less formal and faster than NFA arbitration. Each exchange has a specific set of futures contracts and options listed for trading on the exchange, and the arbitrators tend to have knowledge related to those particular contracts and the exchange rules governing the trading of those particular contracts. NFA has a much broader membership than each exchange, in that NFA members include brokers, advisors, and pool operators who may be dealing with customers in products traded on any U.S. or foreign exchange. As a result, in NFA member arbitration, the knowledge of the panel members may not be as specialized for the dispute as is the case in exchange arbitration. Nevertheless, even where a panel member works in an area of the industry that is different from the area in which the dispute arose, that panel member would be more likely to have knowledge relevant to the dispute than would a judge or jury that is chosen at random.

The characteristics of commodity futures industry arbitration that are not typically present in general commercial arbitration could be incorporated into dispute resolution procedures for other industries. A general arbitration forum or an industry trade association could provide an industry arbitration alternative that could either be incorporated into a pre-dispute arbitration clause or elected by both parties after a dispute arises. Alternatively, individual aspects of commodity futures industry arbitration, such as the limitations on discovery, could be included in optional clauses in arbitrations to be administered by the major ADR providers. The major ADR providers could also make an effort to recruit and include on their selection lists non-lawyer arbitrators in selected industries in order to provide the business perspective to arbitrations involving that industry.

Although member arbitration in the commodity futures industry has many advantages in terms of efficiency and economy, the trade-off is, as with any arbitration process, that the parties have less legal protection. Therefore, any ADR provider or industry considering the adoption of this model should consider whether the commodity futures industry model is appropriate for the industry and also whether there are certain types of cases, based on factors such as the amount in controversy or subject matter, that should be excluded from this model.

Conclusion

Member-to-member arbitration in the commodity futures industry has benefited from its business-oriented procedures that are tailored to the industry. Participants in other industries should consider whether they can also attain such benefits by adopting procedures similar to those in the futures industry.

CHAPTER 12

Sports Arbitration: How and Why It Works; Sports Mediation: How and Why It May Work

Richard W. Pound, Q.C.

EDITOR'S NOTE: Perhaps the most confounding application of Alternative Dispute Resolution is in the context of sports. It is the very nature of athletic competition that adjudications take place. Decisions are made—whether a puck went into a net, whether a pitch was a ball or a strike, whether an elbow was mere contact or a foul—by watchful officials whose participation is the fabric of the match itself. As Richard Pound shows, however, there are layers and layers of conflict in sports—and many ways that non-judicial conflict resolution can come to the rescue.

Arbitration in sports is not a new concept. It has been used for decades, especially in the context of domestic sports-related disputes, many of which have a significant economic importance. Thus, salary disputes, especially those occurring within professional sport associations or leagues, have long been the subject of arbitral proceedings with the consent of all parties. Modern collective bargaining agreements applicable to all of the major professional sports now provide for compulsory arbitration, rather than contemplating recourses before alternative adjudicators such as the regular state or federal courts. The situation is somewhat more complicated when sports-related disputes occur within the context of international sports.

Sports and the Context of Rules

The key to sports—the *sine qua non*—is the governing rules adopted by and accepted by the participants. Without such rules, whatever the activity may be, it is not sport. The rules may be sensible or intuitive and they may also be arbitrary.

The ultimate answer, in some respects, however, is that it really does not matter. What does matter is that the participants have agreed on the rules that will govern their conduct, and that they will determine the outcome of any competition. The rules are a social contract, reflecting the "deal" between the participants. Failure to act in accordance with the rules completely destroys the purpose of the entire competitive exercise and renders it meaningless.

Systemically, therefore, the applicable rules have led to a structure of sport that is coherent and self-contained, capable of self-regulation, and providing due consideration for the health and safety of the participants, while, at the same time, recognizing that the nature of certain sports continues to carry elements of risk of serious injury, or worse.

When organized sport was in its formative stage, in the late nineteenth century, the legal order in society was much less developed than it has now become. The subject matter of the legal order, leaving aside criminal law, was concerned with a limited number of commercial issues and transactions, bills of exchange, protection of property rights, inheritance and rudimentary family law and, of course, constitutional law. Sport was not even on the horizon of the legal order. Sport rules and the administration of sport were entirely private matters, unconnected with the legal system governing society at large. As the legal order expanded to encompass more and more aspects of activity within society and as sport itself expanded in importance, participation, and economic significance, the two systems interacted more and more frequently. Today, sport has all but been subsumed by that order and must now be concerned with carving out those elements in which it can assert and practice responsible autonomy, which includes the resolution of sports-related disputes.

The Resolution of Sports-Related Disputes

The particular challenge, especially in the context of an international sport system, is how to deal effectively with the resolution of disputes that are bound to arise, across a broad canvas that covers more than two hundred jurisdictions and dozens of different sports. There is inevitable disagreement as to the meaning of certain rules, the issue of what constitutes an actionable breach of the rules, the capacity of a party to bring a challenge, choice of law, choice of forum, and the appropriate sanctions when breaches are determined to have occurred. Additional issues include such matters as the eligibility of certain competitors, proper identification of competitors, and corruption or collusion on the part of officials and others. Many of the same issues arise in domestic sport as well, although they may be somewhat less complex than in international sport and less influenced by cultural factors and traditions of conduct and interpretation.

On a purely domestic level, there is an obvious, and traditional, solution. State courts are in place and well-established. They can accept jurisdiction and have the legal capacity to render judgments that are legally effective within their jurisdictions. Thus, whatever finality may be required to bring an end to a dispute can be obtained.

The difficulties inherent in such an approach in the context of sport, even at the domestic level, are that these courts do not have the necessary expertise to deal easily with sport issues. The normal legal process is unsuited to the need for speedy resolution of sports-related disputes, which often require expedited hearings (even in the middle of sport competitions). And many of the litigants (especially athletes) do not have the financial resources to undertake expensive legal proceedings. At the other end of the economic scale, however, there are many well-paid professional athletes, and wealthy team owners, who can easily afford expensive legal fees to defend (or to stifle any attacks upon) what may, in the end, be little more than their economic interests and battered reputations. Prominent examples of this include Lance Armstrong, Barry Bonds, and Alex Rodriguez.

These concerns have led, even domestically, to the choice of arbitration as an alternative, in order to access speed of resolution, flexibility of process, some element of choice in the selection of knowledgeable deciders, and a level of confidentiality that is not available when state courts are the forum for dispute resolution. The well-known insistence on the public nature of legal proceedings as a means of maintaining public confidence in the administration of justice is often at odds with the desire of parties to a dispute to keep private matters private.

At the level of the international sport system, however, there are additional imperatives. Decisions of the regular courts are effective only in the jurisdictions where the judgments are rendered. Absent special or bilateral agreements regarding the enforceability of those judgments, they have no legal effects in other jurisdictions and, to become executory, they must first be confirmed or exemplified by the courts in the other jurisdictions. The practical effect is that the cases may, for all intents and purposes, have to be re-litigated.

Take the example of an athlete who has been suspended by the international federation governing his or her sport, rendering the athlete ineligible to compete in any events organized by or under the authority of that international federation. The suspended athlete then applies to the state courts of his or her country for an Oder that the international federation has acted improperly. Assume the state court rules in favor of the athlete, declaring the athlete eligible to compete and the international federation to have been wrong. Finally, say this happened in Canada. The outcome would be that the athlete would be legally entitled to compete in Canada in certain events—but nowhere else—since the Canadian judgment would be effective only in Canada. This type of conundrum has actually occurred, including in the United States and in Denmark.

Reinstatement demands of this nature are often accompanied by the athlete's claims for damages (loss of income, defamation, damage to repetition, etc.), on which the state courts may also be willing—or required—to rule. There was a well-known case in the United States involving a runner (Butch Reynolds) who was declared ineligible by the international federation, as a consequence of doping. He launched proceedings in the United States in Ohio and obtained a judgment to the effect that not only had he been improperly declared ineligible, but also that as a result of the international federation's libel of him, he had "lost" more than $25 million in prize and sponsorship money. This amount greatly exaggerates any possible amount he might have earned, even had he competed for an entire lifetime.[1]

This was an *ex parte* judgment. The international federation had not bothered to intervene in the domestic proceedings, likely because it did not want to put its jurisdictional authority to discipline athletes to the scrutiny of an American court, which might well be reluctant to find in favor of an international organization at the expense of an American athlete. But, what eventually caught the federation's attention was the possibility that television rights and other fees for certain of its

---

1. *See, e.g.*, DAVID MCARDLE, DISPUTE RESOLUTION IN SPORT: ATHLETES, LAW AND ARBITRATION 43–46 (2014).

events derived from sources within the United States might be garnished by Reynolds. The only pain experienced by many international sports federations is in their wallets. So, it belatedly intervened and was forced to go all the way to the U.S. Supreme Court to get resolution in its favor regarding its authority to discipline athletes for breaches of its rules.[2]

From the perspective of an international sport system, this is completely unsatisfactory. There would be endless local proceedings, a significant likelihood of conflicting judgments, enormous costs, and an overall uncertainty as to which rules and which decisions might apply in any particular circumstance.

Creating an International Sport Arbitral Body

This type of risk led the International Olympic Committee (IOC) to create the Court of Arbitration for Sport (CAS) in 1984, having its seat in Lausanne, Switzerland. The mandate of CAS was to deal with sports-related disputes, mainly within the Olympic Movement. However, it also contemplated accessibility to CAS by non-Olympic sports and parties. Initially, CAS did not deal with decisions rendered by the IOC, which has traditionally held itself out as the supreme authority of the Olympic Movement, but the IOC later agreed that even its own decisions could also be appealed. That decision led to some organizational and governance changes to make certain that CAS could not be perceived as being under the control of the IOC.

From a governance perspective, CAS is now controlled by the International Council of Arbitration for Sport (ICAS). This is a body to which the IOC, the International Federations (IFs) and National Olympic Committees (NOCs) each nominate four members. Those twelve members then select four additional members who are considered to be particularly knowledgeable regarding the concerns of athletes. The sixteen members of ICAS thus chosen then select four additional members with wide experience in international arbitration, to be sure that CAS operates at a level of best procedural practices.

ICAS elects a president, who is also the president of CAS. CAS has two divisions, the Ordinary Arbitration Division and the Appeals Arbitration Division. Each division has a president. The Board of ICAS consists of the president, two vice-presidents, and the presidents of the Ordinary and Appeals Divisions.

---

2. Reynolds v. International Amateur Athletic Federation, 505 U.S. 1301 (1992).

There is a Code of Sports-related Arbitration[3] and Mediation[4] Rules.

A supervisory control over the CAS is exercised by the Swiss Federal Tribunal, the equivalent in Switzerland of the U.S. Supreme Court. That Tribunal has recognized CAS as an independent arbitral tribunal, whose judgments are entitled to deference and, to date, the Tribunal has intervened only where the rules of natural justice (or due process) have not been followed, or where there may have been error as to jurisdiction. It has not attempted to substitute its decision on substantive matters within the competence of CAS.

What is particularly appealing about this level of legal status and professional recognition in the context of international sport (in addition to the consensual nature of the arbitration process itself) is that, by reason of the New York Convention, CAS awards are enforceable in almost all of the major countries. Such enforceability is an essential element in an international sport system, for the reasons arising out of the Butch Reynolds case referred to earlier and the need to have uniform application of sport rules and decisions throughout the world.

The CAS system involves a closed list of arbitrators, selected and appointed by ICAS, for renewable terms of four years, based in part on nominations by stakeholders and in part on recruitment by ICAS among knowledgeable lawyers having both sport and arbitration backgrounds. ICAS establishes a list from which the parties are able to select arbitrators, and the president of each division is authorized to appoint the chairman of arbitral panels, if the party-appointed arbitrators are unable to agree and after consultation with the party-designated arbitrators. While the alternative of permitting parties to nominate whomever they may choose, regardless of sport or legal experience, is occasionally discussed within the ICAS, to date, there has been no concerted challenge to the notion of a closed list. The issue is most often raised when unsuccessful parties to arbitration later attempt to appeal to state courts to vacate an arbitral award.[5]

---

3. http://www.tas-cas.org/en/arbitration/code-procedural-rules.html.
4. http://www.tas-cas.org/en/mediation/rules.html.
5. The Munich Higher Regional Court issued a judgment on 15 January 2015 in Pechstein v. International Skating Union (U1110/14 Kart), which includes comments critical, *inter alia*, of the CAS closed list system. Pechstein's appeal was dismissed by the German Federal Court on June 7, 2016. *See generally,* LawyerIssue, August 15, 2015, http://www.lawyerissue.com/international-arbitration-in-sport-why-the-pechstein-case-could-throw-the-court-of-arbitration-for-sport-into-disarray/.

Since the international sport system is, for all intents and purposes, universally acknowledged, adopted, and enforced, ICAS makes an effort to ensure that the list of arbitrators includes lawyers from all parts of the world, in order to increase the confidence of parties that their particular systems and customs will be understood and acknowledged in arbitration proceedings. This includes ensuring that there is a healthy balance between arbitrators from both civil and common law jurisdictions.

Sport expertise of the adjudicators is one of the hallmarks of CAS arbitrations. Such expertise becomes especially important in arbitrations that take place during competitions, especially major competitions such as the Olympic Games. ICAS establishes what is known as the CAS *ad hoc* Division for the period of the Olympic Games, located in the host city of the Games. It assigns a certain number of arbitrators to the *ad hoc* Division, who are physically present throughout the Games period, along with a designated president of the *ad hoc* Division. As disputes arise, the president immediately establishes panels to hear each case. The special feature of the *ad hoc* Division is that the panels must hear the cases and render written reasoned decisions within 24 hours of the filing of the request for arbitration—sometimes even sooner, if the dispute may affect who participates in an event, say, the following day.

This expeditious appeal process is combined with the provision to athletes of legal services without fee, normally, but not necessarily exclusively, by members of the Bar in the host country.

CAS has taken steps to ensure that it keeps up with technological advances, so that, for example, users can file their documents electronically from anywhere in the world. Hearings can also be held anywhere in the world, at the convenience of the parties. Some can be held on the basis of videoconferencing. CAS even has a fund designated to provide some financial support for athletes (and occasionally other parties) who cannot afford to pay for legal assistance.

In the 30-plus years of its existence, CAS has developed its own jurisprudence and the basic elements of a *lex sportiva* have begun to emerge. This is helpful in developing a consistent approach to similar problems, one that can be relied upon by arbitrators and which can assist the lawyers advising parties to predict with greater certainty the likely outcome of any challenge.

Evidentiary burdens are generally the civil balance of probabilities. Where findings of fact in serious cases, such as in doping, are required, panels make such findings based on the "comfortable satisfaction" of the members of the panel, a burden that is greater than a civil balance of probabilities and less than the criminal burden of proof "beyond a reasonable doubt."

Like other arbitral bodies, CAS has experienced what is termed as the "Americanization" of arbitration, particularly in cases involving doping. Challenges to the appointment of arbitrators are increasing. Discoveries can be abusive. Experts can become advocates. Evidence can be repetitive and unnecessary. Cases can be flooded with procedural motions. Arguments can be endless and irrelevant. Finding the right balance between efficient management of hearings and avoiding any effective denial of procedural fairness requires good judgment and firm management of the process by the chair of any panel.

There is, therefore, something of a parallel universe regarding sports-related disputes, outside the normal system of state courts.

Doping Appeals

Doping appeals tend to attract the most attention among all the cases heard by CAS.

One aspect of this parallel universe just referred to is that administered by the World Anti-Doping Agency (WADA), which was established in 1999 and modeled roughly along governance principles similar to those of CAS. Although WADA was created pursuant to Swiss law, its principal office is located in Montreal. It also has regional offices in Tokyo, Lausanne, Johannesburg, and Montevideo. WADA has a unique hybrid governance structure, in which 50% of its members are state governments and 50% are individuals drawn from the sports movement, the IOC, IFs, NOCs, Olympic athletes, and the International Paralympic Committee. It also has a unique revenue structure under which equal contributions are drawn from governments and the sports movement.

WADA has drafted and adopted the World Anti-Doping Code ("Code"),[6] which in turn has been incorporated, physically or by reference, into the rules of the IOC, every Olympic IF, and every NOC. In the context of sports mediation, discussed below, the process of negotiating the Code was an example of *de facto* mediation. WADA has also worked with governments, under the aegis of UNESCO, to put

---

6. https://www.wada-ama.org/en/resources/the-code/world-anti-doping-code.

in place an International Convention on Doping in Sport, which has now been ratified by some 178 countries, covering almost 99% of the world's population, in which governments agree, among other things, that the Code will be the basis for their actions against doping in sport. The Convention was adopted by the UNESCO Conference of Parties in November 2005 and came into effect upon ratification by thirty member states in early 2006. This is one of the few UNESCO conventions to which the United States is a party.

WADA also ensures, through the Code, that the final arbiter in matters of alleged doping is the CAS and not the state courts in each country. Governments have accepted this position.

How did all this happen? And why would governments surrender the jurisdiction of their state courts on the issue of doping?

In 1998, during the Tour de France, the Festina cycling team was discovered by the French police to be in possession of industrial quantities of doping substances and equipment. It was a huge scandal. There was almost universal recognition that cycling was unwilling or unable to control doping in its own sport, and that this was likely true in other sports as well. The same was true regarding countries being willing to administer stringent doping control over their own athletes. The IOC was seen as too weak to control the worldwide collection of sport organizations, national Olympic committees, and other related agencies making up what is known as the Olympic Movement.

It was against that background that the idea of an independent international anti-doping agency was born. The first World Conference on Doping in Sport was held in early 1999, to generate the consensus that such an agency was required. The stakeholders, both sport and government, moved quickly to establish WADA later that same year, so that it was operational early in 2000, the year of the Olympic Games in Sydney, Australia.

In addition to drafting and adopting the Code, funding research and educational programs, and testing athletes, WADA has the responsibility of monitoring compliance with the Code and of reporting on that compliance. WADA itself cannot sanction anyone. Each responsible organization—such as the IOC for Olympic eligibility, or the International Federations for other competitions such as world championships—has the obligation to impose sanctions in the event of non-compliance. This may involve suspending a country from participation in a particular sport, or even barring a country from taking part in the Olympic Games.

When monitoring individual applications of the Code, WADA has an independent right of appeal to CAS if WADA does not agree with a decision regarding compliance or with a particular sanction when there has been an anti-doping rule violation. This is a very important right and, apart from being able to correct errors, the possibility of such an appeal has a definite deterrent effect on organizations that might otherwise be willing to overlook or under-sanction violators. If those organizational decisions are overturned by CAS, there is a considerable loss of face (failure to be Code-compliant, or being guilty of over-leniency, etc.,) in addition to the costs of another level of appeal.

Governments seem comfortable with doping cases being decided by CAS. The domestic courts, as mentioned earlier, have crowded calendars at best, with delays often measured in years before cases can get to trial, and there is little, if any, experience with the complicated scientific aspects of doping appeals. Such courts, of course, always remain a recourse of last resort for their own citizens claiming a denial of justice or due process, but, absent that aspect, they seem more than willing not only to rely on the CAS expertise, but also to insist that potential challengers must exhaust the obligation to arbitrate before coming to the courts.

A good example of this was Lance Armstrong, who fought to the end to avoid knowledgeable sports arbitration regarding alleged doping infractions, only to be told by the courts (even in his home state of Texas) that he was first required to arbitrate. Faced with that judgment, Armstrong declined to proceed before the arbitrators and folded his litigious tent, not willing to face arbitration. He has now been banned for life from all competition.

He later appeared, as many will recall, on a television program hosted by Oprah Winfrey, to acknowledge, without apparent remorse or repentance, that he had used performance-enhancing drugs and methods throughout his entire competitive career. The only thing about which he seemed regretful was that he had finally been caught. In addition to litigation arising from previous settlements obtained prior to his admission of chronic doping (which have been settled or resulted in judgments rendered against him, in respect of false entitlement to prize money), he now faces extensive litigation, including the prospect of treble damages in respect of a $30 million sponsorship of his cycling team by the U.S. Postal Service, under U.S. whistleblower legislation. The U.S. government has intervened in the action on the side of the whistleblower, Floyd Landis, one of Armstrong's former teammates. What goes around comes around.

CAS and the arbitration conducted under its jurisdiction, at least to date, have served the needs of the stakeholders in international sport quite well. The same would be true of the process of arbitration in sport. This model solution has been adapted by many countries for resolution of sports-related disputes at the domestic level. In Canada, the forum created for such purpose is the Sport Dispute Resolution Centre of Canada (SDRCC).[7] In the United States, there is a somewhat similar process, adopting arbitration under the rules of the American Arbitration Association.[8]

Mediation

Sport came more slowly to the use of mediation as a stand-alone mechanism and to mandatory resolution facilitation as a condition precedent to full arbitration. Perhaps at least part of the reason for the slowness in the adoption of mediation derives from the competitive nature of those involved in sport and the "either-or" mentality that tends to prevail. It is hard to mediate a question of who may have won a sprint, or who may have lifted the heaviest weight.

It is, however, a validation of the mediation process that users are now increasingly likely, in appropriate cases, to see if there may be some middle ground to be found, to recognize that not all cases are clearly all-black or all-white and to avoid the cost and risk of arbitral adjudication of matters that might be concluded with less cost, less time, and more nuance.

As is true in commercial and domestic mediation generally, the real objectives of parties, once identified, may be such that the quasi-judicial outcome of a full arbitration is not necessary. Even in doping cases, while it may not be possible to mediate whether a sample was positive or negative, it can be possible to agree on an appropriate sanction or forward-looking remedial steps, where discretion is permitted under the Code.

Questions of discipline, team selection, funding, and even rule interpretation may also lend themselves to some form of privately negotiated settlement or resolution. There is a growing receptivity to such efforts.

---

7. www.crdsc-sdrcc.ca/eng/home.
8. http://www.usada.org/testing/results/.

Parties may find themselves in effective mediation even without the need for an articulated dispute to provide a formal context. A couple of examples include the description of WADA and the World Anti-Doping Code. The brief description given earlier of the structures may have left an impression that they were nothing but the natural outcomes of the application of common sense to particular problems. But there were deep divisions to be overcome.

The first division related to the governance of WADA. At the World Conference on Doping in Sport, held in Lausanne in February 1999, when the first presentation of an organizational chart of the proposed international agency was made, it had six equal stakeholder groups: The IOC, the IFs, the NOCs, athletes, governments, and an expert group of coaches, event organizers, and someone from the pharma industry.

The timing could hardly have been worse—it was in the middle of the Salt Lake City bidding scandal and the IOC was on the receiving end of endless criticism. When the organogram was first revealed, the governments, which were skeptical of its integrity, collectively rejected it and threatened to leave the conference. They insisted that they should have at least 50% of the voting control.

What looked like a complete disaster turned out to have a silver lining. When asked if they really insisted on 50% voting control, and they said yes, I (having been designated by the IOC to deal with the matter) said, OK, you've got it. They were astonished. But, I said, there were two conditions: One was that we could not afford the glacial pace of normal international government action—we needed to be in the field in less than a year. They agreed.

The second condition was that, if they were going to have a 50% say in governance matters, they must also pay 50% of the costs. You cannot imagine the collective war dance they did on that; some 200 governments squawking about 50% of what might have been $12 million at the beginning of this exciting new venture. We said that if they were not willing to pay their share, they were free to depart, but that we would proceed with the creation of the agency on our own, and would make sure the entire world knew what the governments had done and why. They could not afford that kind of publicity, so we gave them a bit of a way out, by saying that we would pay everything for the first two years and they would find a formula during that period to allow them to start paying their share in year three, which they did, adopting a continental allocation.

Our mutual interests ended up being well-served: We had the governments on board; they got the level of influence they desired; we laid off half the costs of the agency on the shoulders of the stakeholder governments; and governments could now no longer sit back and simply criticize the sports movement regarding drug use in sport. It was a far more satisfactory outcome than the model we had original proposed, and it was the fruit of a quasi-mediative process.

De facto mediation occurred on a sequential basis when, under my presidency, WADA put together what is known as the World Anti-Doping Code. This was a massive project designed to harmonize the many and varied anti-doping rules of more than 200 countries, approximately 100 international sport federations, and approximately 200 NOCs. There was constant consultation, circulation of draft provisions, meetings with different interest groups, mixing and combining both civil and common law drafting styles, responses to suggestions, use of professional facilitators, and consistent but patient persistence. The eventual outcome was a second World Conference in early 2003, at which the Code was adopted with unanimous approval (or at least, without dissent). The outcome was that the single Code now applies to all sports, all countries, and all athletes.

Not all of sport is life-and-death struggles. An amusing personal example of reconciling different interests had its origin in the massive and often unstable egos of some of those in leadership positions within the Olympic Movement. As you may know, there is an accreditation system in place at the Olympic Games, designed partly for security purposes and partly to control access to different sport and official venues. When the system was originally adopted, each category was designated by a letter. "A" was for the IOC, "B" was for international sport federations, "C" was for national Olympic committees, "D" was for organizing committee personnel, "E" was for media, "F" was for athletes, and so forth. It worked fine.

But, some of the sports officials began to complain that the system "discriminated" against them: "B" was inferior to the IOC's "A" category (since they viewed this as a rank order—much like marks at university), and they felt slighted by the unstated suggestion that they were of lesser importance. They insisted on having "A" accreditations as well, to correct this frightful indignity. The IOC was not keen on many of the inherent implications of such a demand. The IOC President described the problem to me and asked for advice as to what to do. I suggested that we change the "A," "B," and "C" accreditations to "IOC,"

"IF," and "NOC" instead. On this basis, the IFs and NOCs could hardly complain that their role at the Games was not properly identified. No ranking was implied, and the accreditation was perfectly descriptive of their roles. If anything, it served to further differentiate the IOC from all the others (since no one else had any idea what the "A" stood for on the accreditation badges). And, as in so many mediations, an outcome was achieved that addressed and incorporated the underlying interests of the disputing parties.

I remember also, in an arbitration in which I served as the panel involving competing factions in taekwondo, that I strongly urged the parties to find a settlement. (In passing, I note that there is often the impression that only about 5% of the fighting in taekwondo seems to occur in competition—all the rest is litigious.) I think what finally drove the parties in my case was that I asked them if they really wanted me to describe their conduct in the written decision that I would be called upon to render. I said that, from what I had already heard, neither party would come off very well and that everyone would know what they had done and what I thought of it. They settled. So, even in the middle of an arbitration, there is still an opportunity to mediate.

The mediation process, even if not fully successful, can neverthe-less be of great assistance in helping the parties identify and agree upon the real issues that need to be decided. All of us have seen contested proceedings that are essentially "primal scream therapy" and which have everything but the kitchen sink thrown in for apparent good measure. A good mediator can narrow the issues and help sort out the facts that really matter; dispose of issues that the parties agree upon, or that are not essential to determine, or that fall outside the scope of the proceedings; identify and narrow the evidence that should be adduced; and focus the argument or submissions. Even in doping cases, while you cannot mediate your way out of a positive test, you may be able to agree upon an appropriate sanction for the infraction, including start and stop dates.

In the Canadian sports arbitration system, there is a mandatory resolution facilitation process as a condition to eventual arbitration.

All that said, there may be occasions when the IOC, as an interna-tional self-governing organization, wants to avoid mediation or even pseudo-mediation. One such time was in relation to the Salt Lake City bidding scandal in 1999. The U.S. Congress was mounted on a moral high horse and wanted to summon the IOC and, particularly, the IOC President, to appear before one or more of its committees in response to the scandal. The Congress has a tendency to wrap itself in an impenetrable cloak of moral rectitude and, at least to Canadian eyes, this was one of those times. On this occasion, it had decided that only Congress was capable of directing the IOC in matters of good governance (drawing, no doubt, on its own impeccable self-regulatory experience).

Had the IOC gone before a congressional committee at that time, there was little doubt that we would have been lectured about our bad behavior and informed of the governance changes we were expected to make. The two United States members of the IOC gave testimony and were given a very rough ride by the committee. While never actually issued, the IOC was threatened with the issuance of a subpoena to appear.

Our strategy was that, under no circumstances, would we negotiate any possible governance reforms with the U.S. Congress. Instead, we conducted the process on our own, with many leading world figures involved, put the reforms in place, and only then agreed that our president would appear, to describe how we had put our own house in order. Congress, faced with this and supportive testimony from influential Americans, had little alternative but to acknowledge a meaningful reform process by the IOC, and the crisis passed.

Enlisting Outside Help

Given the extensive involvement of sponsors in sport, both domestic and international, professional and amateur, many question whether such involvement depends to some, if any, degree on the underlying integrity of the sport. The answer is likely what one might expect—yes and no.

In the Olympic context, the IOC has worked very hard to stress the aspirational goals of striving to do one's best, fair play, peace, non-discrimination, doping-free sport, and similar elements. It has been reasonably successful in creating an Olympic brand that resonates on a worldwide basis, with remarkable consistency. Sponsors support those values because their customers and potential customers support them and are willing to pay a bit more for their goods or services if they are connected with the Olympic brand. The Olympic Movement deliberately differentiates the Olympic "product" from that offered by the professional or entertainment sport organizations and leagues. Using doping as an example, compare the concern with a positive test in the Olympics with a positive test in virtually any professional sport.

In the Olympics, there is inordinate disappointment, because doping is incompatible with the ideals of the Games. In many professional sports (assuming the testing programs are properly implemented), no one seems to care. Everyone involved should care about it, because every athlete using drugs is someone's child and because there is economic fraud practiced against clean athletes and against the spectating public, which has been led to believe that there are effective anti-doping policies in place.

Because sponsorship involves image transfer and association, in recent years, some sponsors have begun to realize that it is not good for their image to be associated with certain individuals, organizations, sports, or events if unacceptable conduct is involved. They have begun to include "morals" clauses in some of their contracts, which enable them to terminate the contract, reduce what is paid, and even recover what they have paid in the event the described conduct occurs. The IOC experienced this in the wake of the Salt Lake City crisis. I was then responsible for all of the IOC's marketing activities and fully understood the reason why our sponsors might want such a clause, and I had no objection to including it in our agreements. In addition, we also learned that we might wish, in certain circumstances, to be able to terminate our relationship with sponsors whose corporate conduct we found to be objectionable and requested, in turn, similar rights.

The next step—namely, approaching sponsors to use their leverage to ensure that good governance is practiced by all sponsored individuals, organizations, sports and events as a condition of sponsorship—has not yet become the norm. It is interesting, in the context of the most recent scandal affecting the Fédération Internationale de Football Association (FIFA), that one sponsor, The Coca-Cola Company, has called for an independent inquiry into the allegations of corruption, money laundering, and other criminal activities. More interesting will be the actions of other sponsors and, of course, FIFA itself. A concerted withdrawal of sponsor support would undoubtedly have an impact on FIFA, which, like many sport organizations, has a tendency to feel pain only in its wallet. This will be a work in progress. Thus far, FIFA shows no inclination to have an independent inquiry and proposes to establish yet another task force to replace an earlier one which had failed to identify and solve the allegations of corruption, especially as to the selection of Russia and Qatar as the host countries of the World Cup in 2018 and 2022 respectively.

In addition, one would need to have appropriate contractual language to create a right on the part of sponsors to intervene and to initiate arbitral proceedings. Presumably, the language that could trigger the right to withdraw would likely fall short of requiring a sponsor to make out a case of fraud or corruption, but would focus on concerns such as damage to reputation or governance failures arising from selection of host cities or commercial dealings on the part of the organization.

There is certainly potential in such an approach, especially since it might relieve the pressure on members of the organization who may be reluctant to become or to appear as whistleblowers. Treatment of whistleblowers is often harsher than the treatment of the offending member or participant.

CHAPTER 13

The Delaware Rapid Arbitration Act

Blake Rohrbacher[1]

EDITOR'S NOTE: Delaware is the unrivaled center of corporate formation, and its courts have long been acknowledged as the preeminent forum for corporate governance and business decisions. It is therefore fitting that this volume ends with an analysis of the most recent, and most innovative, state statute to attempt to satisfy business expectations of a method of resolution of commercial disputes that is final, swift, inexpensive, informed, and rational.

On April 2, 2015, the State of Delaware adopted the Delaware Rapid Arbitration Act (the "DRAA" or the "Act"), an innovative approach to dispute resolution. As explained further below, the DRAA was intended to improve on traditional arbitration by streamlining the beginning, middle, and end of the arbitration process.[2] Delaware thus offers to its corporate citizens an effective and cost-efficient method of resolving their disputes in a customizable and confidential setting.

This chapter explores the features of the Act that distinguish it from traditional arbitral regimes and provides an overview of practice under the Act.

---

1. Opinions expressed in this chapter are those of the author and not necessarily those of Richards, Layton & Finger, P.A. or its clients.

2. *See generally* Blake Rohrbacher, *Introducing Delaware's Rapid Arbitration Act*, INSIGHTS, 6 (May 2015). Additional information regarding the Act may be found at www.rlf.com/DRAA.

Origins of the DRAA

The DRAA was Delaware's second major attempt at an innovative approach to dispute resolution. In 2009, Delaware's General Assembly adopted an arbitration statute providing the Court of Chancery with the power to arbitrate business disputes—confidentially and quickly—in front of sitting members of the Court.[3] Due in part to the Court of Chancery's reputation as the leading business law court in the United States, the new statute attracted a number of Chancery arbitrations in its first year of effectiveness.

The statute was nonetheless successfully challenged in the federal courts. A divided panel of the U.S. Court of Appeals for the Third Circuit held that Delaware's Chancery arbitration statute was unconstitutional on the basis that the public had a right of access to such proceedings.[4]

So Delaware looked for other ways to improve on dispute resolution. A working group, led by Delaware's Chief Justice Leo E. Strine Jr., Chancellor Andre G. Bouchard, and Secretary of State Jeffrey W. Bullock, was created to study current arbitration systems. After consulting with national and international arbitration practitioners and experts, the working group identified particular issues with traditional arbitral regimes, including the length of time to decision and the parties' opportunities to hinder resolution.

Although Delaware had enacted its own version of the Uniform Arbitration Act,[5] the working group decided to draft a new arbitration statute. Thus, the DRAA was born, expressly designed to allow litigants a flexible, efficient, and binding arbitral process that avoids the delay possible in other arbitral regimes.

Requirements for Invoking the DRAA

The DRAA offers parties a means to obtain efficient and expedited arbitration. To accomplish this goal, parties must waive a number of rights and procedural protections that they would otherwise have. Accordingly, the Act requires that the parties make a knowing and unequivocal choice to accept the DRAA regime.

---

3. DEL. CODE. ANN. tit. 10 § 349.

4. Strine v. Del. Coalition. for Open Gov't., Inc., 733 F.3d 510 (3d Cir. 2013), *cert. denied*, 134 S. Ct. 1511 (2014).

5. DEL. CODE. ANN. tit. 10 § 5701 *et seq.*

To arbitrate under the Act, parties must execute a written agreement to submit to arbitration under the DRAA. To be effective, this arbitration agreement must include "an express reference to the 'Delaware Rapid Arbitration Act.'"[6] Simply stating, for example, that the parties agree to a "prompt arbitration under Delaware law" may not suffice.

The DRAA specifically requires that the arbitration agreement be "signed by the parties" to the arbitration.[7] This requirement ensures that no person can be forced to arbitrate under the DRAA without express consent. Thus, a corporation may not bind its stockholders to DRAA arbitration simply by adopting a DRAA arbitration provision in its bylaws. For similar reasons, and to avoid its use in contracts of adhesion, the DRAA may not be used in agreements with a "consumer."[8] In short, the DRAA is intended for sophisticated parties who mutually and intentionally agree to invoke its terms.

Use of the DRAA is also limited to certain types of parties. At least one party to the arbitration agreement must be a business entity, which includes nearly any type of corporation or unincorporated entity, such as a statutory trust, limited liability company, or limited partnership. This business entity must be organized or formed under Delaware law or have its principal place of business in Delaware.

Further, although the parties may agree that certain aspects of their relationship, or other rights and obligations, may be governed by any law they choose, the DRAA requires that the arbitration agreement itself must be governed by Delaware law. For example, the parties might enter into a joint-venture agreement governing an entity in Brazil with the licensing provisions governed by local law and enforceable in Brazil's courts, while the governance provisions are governed by Delaware law and subject to DRAA arbitration in Rio de Janeiro.

Although the parties to an arbitration agreement need not designate an arbitrator in their agreement, some arbitrator must accept appointment before an arbitration under the DRAA may commence. The Act provides parties with significant flexibility in this regard. First, the parties may name a particular arbitrator in the arbitration agreement. For example, the parties may identify a specific individual (for example, "Judge Jones") or a specific entity (for example, "ABC Accounting Firm") in their arbitration agreement. Second, the parties may provide a method in the agreement under which an

---

6. DEL. CODE ANN. tit. 10 § 5803(a)(5).
7. DEL. CODE ANN. tit. 10 § 5803(a)(1).
8. DEL. CODE ANN. tit. 10 § 5803(a)(3); *see also* 6 DEL. CODE ANN. tit. 6 § 2731(1).

arbitrator may be selected: The parties could agree on a procedure for selecting arbitrators (for example, "each party will select an arbitrator, and those two arbitrators will select a third") or could agree on certain qualifications to guide the parties' selection of an arbitrator in the future (for example, "the arbitrator must be a CPA with 10 years' work experience"). Third, the parties may simply agree to designate an arbitrator later, even if their agreement is silent as to any method of choosing an arbitrator. Fourth, if the parties did not or cannot agree on an arbitrator, or if an agreed-on arbitrator cannot or will not serve, the Court of Chancery of the State of Delaware may appoint an arbitrator in a special proceeding (described below).

The Effect of Invoking the DRAA

As noted above, the expedited and streamlined processes that make the DRAA unique require parties to give up a number of rights and consent to a number of conditions. Accordingly, the entry into an arbitration agreement governed by the DRAA triggers a number of consequences: The parties to such an agreement are deemed to have consented to, among other things, (1) the DRAA's arbitration procedures; (2) the arbitrator's exclusive jurisdiction to determine issues of substantive and procedural arbitrability; (3) the exclusive personal and subject matter jurisdiction of an arbitration, regardless of where the hearing is held; and (4) the exclusive personal and subject matter jurisdiction of the Delaware courts (but only for limited purposes, as provided in the DRAA). Similarly, parties to an arbitration agreement under the DRAA waive, among others, the right to enjoin any arbitrations under the DRAA; the right to remove to a federal court any judicial proceeding under the DRAA; the right to appeal an arbitrator's interim awards; and the right to challenge or appeal an arbitrator's final award, except as provided in the DRAA.

Rapid at the Beginning: Arbitrability and the Appointment Procedure

The Act is designed to prevent lawsuits seeking to enjoin the arbitration. These injunction suits often challenge "substantive arbitrability" (that is, whether certain claims are subject to arbitration) and "procedural arbitrability" (that is, whether one party complied with the terms of the arbitration agreement). The DRAA prevents parties from engaging in such battles by, as noted above, providing that parties to an arbitration agreement under the Act have consented to submit these issues exclusively to the arbitrator and have waived the right to bring these issues to court or to seek to enjoin arbitration under the Act. Accordingly, arbitrations commenced under the DRAA should proceed promptly, without the risk of delay through injunction proceedings.

The DRAA is also designed to help arbitrations get underway quickly. If the parties are unable to agree on an arbitrator, or if an agreed-on arbitrator is unable or unwilling to serve, the Act provides a special procedure through which the parties may seek the assistance of the Delaware Court of Chancery. Any party may initiate this proceeding to appoint an arbitrator. After the proceeding begins, all parties propose up to three potential arbitrators each. To address any concerns of favoritism, the parties must submit to the Court a joint list of potential arbitrators (and background information regarding the potential arbitrators) without indicating which party is proposing which arbitrator.[9] Given the limited time frame available for decision, the Court's choice of an arbitrator is constrained, and an arbitrator appointed by the Court must be (a) named in (or selected under) the terms of the arbitration agreement; (b) an expert in a non-legal discipline described in the arbitration agreement (for example, an expert in the textile industry); or (c) a senior Delaware lawyer. The Court of Chancery must appoint an arbitrator within 30 days after service of the initiating petition, and this appointment may not be appealed.

Rapid in the Middle: Discovery and the Arbitrator's Deadline

The most innovative feature of the DRAA involves its mechanism for enforcing the deadlines of arbitrations under the Act. Arbitration hearings under the DRAA generally proceed as would most other arbitrations, but the DRAA seeks to ensure rapid resolution through its default 120-day limit. Although the parties are free to agree otherwise

---

9. *See* Del. Ct. Ch. R. 96(d).

before the arbitration commences, arbitrations under the Act must result in a final award "within 120 days of the arbitrator's acceptance of the arbitrator's appointment."[10] The parties, with the arbitrator's consent, may jointly extend this period by up to (but no more than) 60 additional days. This deadline is strictly enforced through a sliding-scale reduction in the arbitrator's fee; the fee is reduced with the lateness of the arbitrator's final award. That is, if the arbitrator issues a final award less than 30 days late, between 30 and 60 days late, or more than 60 days late, the arbitrator's fees are reduced by 25%, 75%, and 100%, respectively.[11] This structure is intended to provide an incentive to arbitrators for providing timely resolutions and for exercising tight control over the parties in the arbitration. Moreover, arbitrators issuing late final awards must self-report to the Court of Chancery, which may then take that report into account when making future arbitrator appointments.

The Act also contains a number of minor innovations designed to keep arbitrations moving smoothly. First, the arbitrator's interim rulings (whether those involve, for example, arbitrability determinations, interim equitable relief and sanctions, or discovery rulings) may not be appealed. That prevents piecemeal challenges that would tend to delay or disrupt the arbitration. Second, the arbitrator may retain appropriate counsel, in consultation with the parties, and that counsel may make rulings on issues of law on the arbitrator's behalf. That feature of the Act streamlines arbitrations and allows non-lawyer arbitrators to address purely legal issues if those arise. Third, the parties are entitled to set the scope of pre-hearing discovery, and third-party discovery is not allowed unless the parties agree. The limitation on third-party discovery ensures the speed and confidentiality of arbitrations under the Act. If third-party discovery is allowed, the arbitrator is empowered to seek enforcement of subpoenas in the Court of Chancery. Finally, the parties to an arbitration agreement may agree—with the arbitrator's consent—to amend an arbitration agreement to alter the procedures of the arbitration if they later determine that a different structure would better suit the dispute. The only exception to that feature involves the deadline for the arbitration; as noted above, the arbitration deadline may be extended by only 60 days after the arbitration begins.

---

10. DEL. CODE ANN. tit. 10 § 5808(b).

11. In certain limited circumstances, the arbitrator may petition the Court of Chancery to reverse the effect of the statutory reduction in fees, but the arbitrator must make a powerful showing to obtain this result.

Rapid at the End: Deemed Confirmation and Direct Challenges

The final arbitral award must be in writing and must be signed by the arbitrator; it must also provide a form of judgment for entry by a court under the Act. Following the issuance of a final award, the Act includes two innovations designed to enhance the finality of an arbitration.

First, the final award need not be subject to contentious (and often inefficient) confirmation proceedings in a trial court. If no challenge to the final award is raised by the fifth business day after the time period for a challenge expires, the DRAA provides that the final award is deemed to be confirmed. That is, no party need bring confirmation proceedings. Instead, either party may seek a prompt final judgment from the appropriate Delaware court on this confirmed final award.

Second, by default, if one party wishes to challenge a final award, the challenge must be taken within 15 days. The default under the DRAA is that any challenge goes straight to the Delaware Supreme Court, which will consider the challenge under the limited grounds for obtaining vacation, modification, or correction of an arbitral award under the Federal Arbitration Act ("FAA").[12] This challenge would be public and subject to the Supreme Court Rules. The parties to an arbitration agreement governed by the Act may also contractually waive appellate review or agree to an arbitral appeal. If the parties agree to an arbitral appeal, they may opt for a different standard of appellate review.[13] The DRAA expressly allows this flexibility.

Together, these innovations are designed to provide the prevailing party in a DRAA arbitration with a final and enforceable judgment as promptly as possible.

---

12. 9 U.S.C. § 1 *et seq.*

13. That is, the parties may agree to a standard of review other than that provided in the FAA only if they agree to an arbitral appeal. Any challenge to a DRAA arbitration that goes to court (which, by statute, must be the Delaware Supreme Court) is subject to the standards set forth in the FAA. *See* DEL. CODE ANN. tit. 10 § 5809(c); *see also* Hall St. Assocs., L.L.C. v. Mattel, Inc., 552 U.S. 576 (2008) (holding that judicial review of an arbitration subject to the FAA is to be governed by the standards in the FAA).

Drafting Considerations

Given the express requirements in the DRAA, one practitioner hand-book provides (although does not recommend) the following clause as the "bare minimum" necessary for an arbitration agreement, so long as one of the parties to the agreement is a Delaware corporation or other business entity and none is a "consumer" under the meaning of the Act:

> The parties hereby agree to arbitrate any and all disputes arising under or related to this agreement, including disputes related to the interpretation of this agreement, under the Delaware Rapid Arbitration Act. This provision shall be governed by Delaware law, without reference to the law chosen for any other provision(s) of this agreement.[14]

Given the Act's flexibility, any person considering a DRAA provision in an agreement should carefully consider the many options available to make the choices that best suit the parties' situations.

Among the specific issues that should be considered when drafting an arbitration agreement are the following: the method of choosing the arbitrator, the availability of third-party discovery, the time limit for the arbitration, the appellate procedure for the arbitration, and the rules that govern the arbitration. To the last point, the Delaware Supreme Court has promulgated default rules to govern DRAA arbitrations,[15] but the parties are free to select any different rules they wish, so long as they are not inconsistent with the Act's terms. Each of these aspects may be customized by the parties to an arbitration agreement to ensure that the arbitral process under the DRAA is best suited to resolve their particular disputes.

In short, the DRAA allows for a flexible and efficient mode of dispute resolution, different from traditional arbitral regimes in its several innovative mechanisms to avoid delay at each stage of the arbitration process. As such, the Act is worthy of consideration by parties and practitioners negotiating arbitration provisions.

---

14. Gregory V. Varallo, Blake Rohrbacher & John D. Hendershot, The Practitioner's Guide to the Delaware Rapid Arbitration Act 65 (2d ed. 2015), www.rlf.com/DRAA.
15. *See* http://www.rlf.com/DRAA/OfficialRules/.

About the Contributors

Timothy R. Bow is an Associate at the law firm of Markowitz, Ringel, Trusty & Hartog in Miami.

Howard Brod Brownstein is a Certified Turnaround Professional and President of The Brownstein Corporation in Conshohocken, PA.

Paulette Brown, Partner and co-chair of the firmwide Diversity & Inclusion Committee at Locke Lord LLP, is president of the American Bar Association. Brown has repeatedly been named as a New Jersey Super Lawyer and by *US News* as one of the Best Lawyers in America in the area of commercial litigation. Brown earned her J.D. at Seton Hall University School of Law and her B.A. at Howard University.

Louis F. Burke has a small boutique litigation and arbitration practice in NYC specializing in complex trading disputes and market manipulation class actions. He is co-chair of the ABA Section of Litigation Alternate Dispute Resolution Committee and co-chair of the ABA Section of Dispute Resolution Arbitration Committee. He has co-authored and edited *Alternate Dispute Resolution in the Futures Industry*, Juris Publications 2013. He has been voted to be on the list of Super Lawyers and Best Lawyers in America in securities litigation and commercial litigation, respectively.

Hugh Christie, LL.B. (Queen's), LL.M. (London) is the Managing Partner of Ogletree Deakins International, LLP, Toronto office. He has 35 years of experience advising public and private sector employers on the full range of issues that arise in the workplace. He has been a member of Canada's delegation to the International Labour Organization and is Co-Chair of the Centre for Law in the Contemporary Workplace, at the Queen's University Faculty of Law.

Kristine Dorrain, Esq. is an ADR attorneys at Forum , a national ADR service provider located in Minneapolis. Ms. Dorrain is licensed to practice law in the state of Minnesota and has focused her legal career on intellectual property and ADR and is a certified neutral in the state of Minnesota.

Ryan Isenberg is a Shareholder in the firm of Isenberg & Hewitt, P.C., in Atlanta. His practice is devoted to complex commercial litigation involving trademarks, copyrights, trade secrets, employment restrictive covenants, "partnership" disputes, and creditor's rights matters both in and out of bankruptcy. He has represented parties ranging in size from mom-and-pop businesses to large publicly held corporations in various state and federal courts around the country, in addition to having litigated before the Trademark Trial and Appeal Board and arbitrated national and international domain name disputes.

Stephen H. Knee, Esq., ABA Business Law Section, Dispute Resolution Committee and Mergers and Acquisitions Committee, Member. Mr. Knee is of Counsel with Greenbaum, Rowe, Smith & Davis, LLP, Roseland, NJ.

John Levitske, CPA/ABV/CFF/CGMA, ASA, CFA, CFLC, CIRA, MBA, JD, is a Senior Director in the Commercial Dispute Advisory Services practice of Huron Consulting Group, Chicago, Illinois. He has more than 30 years of experience in business valuation, forensic accounting, and merger & acquisition disputes; has testified as an expert witness in the U.S. and Europe in depositions, trials, hearings, and international arbitration; and has also served as a neutral arbitrator. In addition, he is Vice Chair of the Dispute Resolution Committee of the American Bar Association's Business Law Section and National Immediate Past President of the Forensic Expert Witness Association.

Jerry M. Markowitz is a Shareholder at the law firm of Markowitz, Ringel, Trusty & Hartog in Miami.

Sylvia Mayer, the founding member of S. Mayer Law PLLC, focuses her practice primarily on mediation, arbitration, civil litigation and business bankruptcy. She mediates and arbitrates disputes of all kinds, including, business, bankruptcy, civil, commercial, consumer, elder and adult care, labor and employment, financial services, insurance, personal injury, and workouts. With more than 20 years of legal experience in civil litigation, commercial bankruptcy, out of court workouts, and financial institution advisory services, Ms. Mayer has represented plaintiffs, defendants, debtors, committees, trustees, financial institutions, and other parties in state and federal courts around the country. She has also counseled parties on issues related to business transactions and represented companies and their stakeholders in out of court workouts.

William J. Nissen is a partner of Sidley Austin LLP in Chicago and is Chairman of the Private Litigation Subcommittee of the ABA Committee on Derivatives and Futures Regulation. His practice focuses on regulation and litigation involving the derivatives and futures industries. He has tried numerous arbitrations at the National Futures Association and the various futures exchanges. He was named the *Best Lawyers'* 2013 Chicago, Derivatives and Futures law "Lawyer of the Year."

Sandra Partridge, Esq. is an ADR attorney at Forum , a national ADR service provider located in Minneapolis. She is licensed to practice law in Pennsylvania and holds a Juris Doctorate from the Dickinson School of Law of the Pennsylvania State University, where she focused her legal studies on arbitration and mediation. Sandra is also a graduate of the Cornell ILRB Mediation program. She was Vice President of the New York office of the American Arbitration Association before joining Forum.

F. Peter Phillips is a commercial arbitrator and mediator in Montclair, NJ. He is Director of the Alternative Dispute Resolution Skills Program and Adjunct Professor at New York Law School. He is former Chair of the ABA Business Law Section Dispute Resolution Committee. Further information is available at www.BusinessConflictManagement.com.

Richard W. Pound is a Canadian lawyer who specializes in tax as well as commercial and sports arbitration. He is a member of the International Council of Arbitration for Sport and is a frequent arbitrator for the Sport Dispute Resolution Center of Canada. He is a former Business Law Advisor in the Business Law Section of the ABA.

Blake Rohrbacher's practice includes litigation as well as advisory and transactional matters relating to Delaware corporations and alternative entities. A graduate of Yale Law School, Mr. Rohrbacher has authored a number of publications regarding Delaware corporate law and litigation practice, and he has been recognized in Benchmark Litigation, Super Lawyers and Chambers USA. Mr. Rohrbacher serves on the Delaware Court of Chancery Rules Committee.

Joseph Semo is director of Semo Law Group, Washington, DC. Mr. Semo advises clients with respect to compensation and employee benefits matters including institutional investment issues and fiduciary issues. Mr. Semo earned his undergraduate degree from the Wharton School of the University of Pennsylvania and his law degree from George Washington University. He is member of the bar of the District of Columbia, Maryland, Virginia, and Wisconsin. He is admitted to numerous federal district courts and circuit courts and the United States Supreme Court.

Scott Y. Stuart is Founder and Co-CEO of Esquify.com, a document review firm in Chicago.

Index

Arbitrator's deadline (Delaware Rapid Arbitration Act), 148

Armstrong, Lance, 127, 134–135

Asset Purchase Agreement (M&As), 68–69

Authority to settle, in public infrastructure project disputes, 114–115

Avoidances (bankruptcy), 57–58

Awards
    in ADR clauses, 34–35
    appealing, 83
    Delaware Rapid Arbitration Act, 148–149

B

Bankruptcy Code, 50, 56–57

Bankruptcy mediation, 49–61
    best practices in, 51–52
    in consumer bankruptcy contexts, 58
    Financial Advisor's role in, 56–58
    in mortgage modification mediation, 58–60
    use of joint session and caucus in, 53–56

Baseball Arbitration, 18–19

BATNA (best alternative to a negotiated agreement), 11, 14

"The big room," 103

Binding arbitration
    of employment-related disputes, 46
    in M&As, 70–71
    for privately owned business disputes, 83

Bonds, Barry, 127

Bouchard, Andre G., 144

Bounded Arbitration, 19

Breaches of seller's representations and warranties disputes (M&As), 66–67

Bullock, Jeffrey W., 144

Business "divorces." *See* Privately owned businesses

Buy-sell provisions, in shareholders' agreements, 79–81

C

Canada
    Sport Dispute Resolution Centre of Canada, 135
    sports arbitration system, 138

CAS (Court of Arbitration for Sport), 129–135

Case law, 31–32

Caucus
    in bankruptcy mediation, 53–56
    in nonbankruptcy mediations, 53

Chapter 11 bankruptcy, 56–57, 61

Chicago Board of Trade, 120

Chicago Mercantile Exchange, 120

Chief Restructuring Officer (CRO), 56, 57

Circuit City Stores, Inc. v. Adams, 41

Civil cases, 4

Client counseling, pre-mediation, 12

Client's business needs, 31

Co-location, for public infrastructure projects, 103

The Coca-Cola Company, 140

Cognitive barriers, 12–13

Cognitive dissonance, 13

Collective bargaining agreements (sports), 125

Commercial arbitration, 7, 119–124
    in commodity futures industry, 120–124
    industry-specific, 119
    lawyer and non-lawyer arbitrators in, 121

Commercial dispute management clauses, 27–35
    and ADR as management tool, 29–31
    design of, 31–32